How to Trap and Snare

A complete Manual for the Sportsman, Game Preserver, Gamekeeper, and Amateur

by
William Carnegie "Moorman"

Read Country Books
Home Farm
44 Evesham Road
Cookhill, Alcester
Warwickshire
B49 5LJ

ISBN No. 1-905124-03-1

First Published: 1898
Published by Read Books 2004

British Library Cataloguing-in-Publication Data
A catalogue record for this book is available
from the British Library.

Read Country Books
Home Farm
44 Evesham Road
Cookhill, Alcester
Warwickshire
B49 5LJ

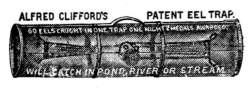

HOW TO TRAP AND SNARE

A Complete Manual for the Sportsman, Game Preserver, Gamekeeper, and Amateur

ON

THE ART OF TAKING ANIMALS AND BIRDS IN TRAPS, SNARES, AND NETS.

WITH NUMEROUS ILLUSTRATIONS.

BY

WILLIAM CARNEGIE ("Moorman"),

Author of "Practical Game Preserving," Etc.

LONDON:
PRINTED AND PUBLISHED
AT THE OFFICES OF THE "SHOOTING TIMES," 72-77 TEMPLE-CHAMBERS.
FLEET-STREET, E.C.

CONTENTS.

INTRODUCTORY 1
CHAPTER I.—The Dorset Trap and its Varieties 4
CHAPTER II.—Humane Traps 15
CHAPTER III.—Tools, etc., for Trapping 21
CHAPTER IV.—How to set the Dorset Trap 24
CHAPTER V.—Round and Small Steel Traps 34
CHAPTER VI.—How to set Round and Small Vermin Traps... 42
CHAPTER VII.—Rabbit Trapping 47
CHAPTER VIII.—Trapping Ground Vermin 62
CHAPTER IX.—Rats 76
CHAPTER X.—Rats (continued) 90
CHAPTER XI.—Wild Cats 99
CHAPTER XII.—Poaching Dogs and Cats 104
CHAPTER XIII.—Trapping Foxes 109
CHAPTER XIV.—Trapping Hawks 120
CHAPTER XV.—Trapping Crows, Rooks, etc. 127
CHAPTER XVI.—Trapping Magpies and Jays... 133
CHAPTER XVII.—Box, Cage, and other Traps 142
CHAPTER XVIII.—The Snare and its Varieties 163
CHAPTER XIX.—The Use of the Snare 169
CHAPTER XX.—General Trapping and Snaring 178
CHAPTER XXI.—Pitfalls 185
CHAPTER XXII.—Springes and Hingles 188
CHAPTER XXIII.—Nets and their Employment 197
CHAPTER XXIV.—Nets and their Employment (continued). 208
CHAPTER XXV.—Moles and how to catch them ... 212
CHAPTER XXVI.—Trapping Fishery Pests 217

PREFACE.

THIS Manual is intended to provide as much practical insight into the various modes of trapping, snaring, and netting the animals and birds of the British Isles as can be furnished by writing.

Wherever possible and desirable, such insight is given of the haunts and habits of the creatures to be caught as may prove useful to the amateur or tyro, for whom it is more particularly planned, than for the professional.

Every piece of work, device, trap, snare, or net described has been performed, employed, or made by the author, and it is hoped that the experience gained during many years may prove of advantage to others who may be induced to follow the Art of the Trapper, either for pastime or profit.

For Healthy Broods

SPRATT'S PATENT

GAME FOODS

Samples Post Free, also New Illustrated Catalogue of Game Foods and Appliances, with chapters on the various branches of Game Rearing.

SPRATT'S PATENT, LTD.,
24 & 25 Fenchurch Street, London, E.C.

How to Trap and Snare.

INTRODUCTORY.

WHEREVER game is preserved, vermin must be destroyed; in fact, as that great sporting writer, "Idstone," was wont to put it, "to destroy vermin is to preserve game." At the time he wrote, but little of the science to which modern game-preserving has attained was known; but the axiom he laid down holds good to-day as it did then, and the destruction of vermin remains an ever-important item in the itinerary of the game preserver's progress. The art of trapping and snaring, however, together with the use of nets in a legitimate manner, is one with which the general sportsman appears content to maintain but a very superficial acquaintance, and even the latter-day game-keeper is very usually content to relegate such matters to his under-men or the professional vermin-catcher, passing it off as a minor kind of accomplishment. It is, however, nothing of the sort, and, although the mere setting of a trap or laying of a snare may appear a very simple affair of itself, skill in the handling (which includes concealment), art in the time and place of employment, and choice of the form of trap, snare, or wile play such an important part in influencing success or failure that to become a success-

B

ful and certain trapper involves an amount of experience, insight, and skill far greater than is necessary in the rearing of game or the shooting of it when reared.

In the first place, an infinitely more correct knowledge of every detail of the features of the haunts and habits of the quarry to be taken in trap or snare is required than is the case where the preservation or shooting of ordinary items of fur and feather is concerned. The mere putting down of a trap, a snare, a fall, or a hingle without full knowledge of what has to be caught and what has to be done to catch it will not lead, probably, to anything at all. The skilled trapper knows exactly what he intends to capture, how he will take it, and, approximately, when he will take it. To accomplish this he must possess not only an intimate acquaintance with the form and habits of the creature he seeks to capture, but also of the woodcraft incidental to its surroundings. These items of knowledge are not gained from haphazard acquaintance, hearsay, or teaching; they can only be acquired at the expenditure of time and trouble intelligently applied, keen insight into animal ways, and the exercise of much patience and skill.

It is possible for the tyro to gain a large amount of information from the written instructions and experiences of others, but to prove successful he must be assiduous in himself, observing all the incidences of the bird and animal life amongst which he proposes to work: he must be early and late afield, a careful observer of the weather, its changes and portents, and be satisfied to put up with its inclemencies, and not infrequently take advantage of them. It is, moreover, of the first importance to persevere, trying again and again, maybe, before ultimate success is assured. The amateur trapper or snarer is certain to find himself frequently at fault at first. He may put two and two together with extraordinary apparent exactitude, and find the sum total of his endeavours entirely out of his reckoning; but, sooner or later, a correct solution of every difficulty comes, and that intuitive knowledge of what to do and how to do it is acquired, and the tyro merges into the expert.

In the chapters which follow, the various manufactured traps will be described and referred to in their most practical and adaptable forms, the making of others, of snares, hingles, falls, and the like described, and as much instruction as to their employment given as will serve to initiate the inexperienced into their use and application.

It may be imagined that trapping and snaring are an uninteresting kind of drudgery very necessary, but outside the amateur's sphere of interest. On the contrary, it is an engaging and fascinating pursuit, and one worthy the skill and attention of those to whom country life in general, and game-preserving in particular, possess a never-ending attraction.

It may be said that it is cruel. Sport in whatever form entails relative cruelty. The true sportsman reduces it to its minimum, and the good trapper pursues a precisely similar object. It is only the careless, clumsy, lazy user of traps and snares who is needlessly cruel; the efficient workman is never needlessly so. Nature in her own methods is ofttimes far more unrelentingly cruel than man, and the most cruel of her creatures are the predatory ones against which the trapper wages war.

CHAPTER I.

THE DORSET TRAP AND ITS VARIETIES.

We have in the up-to-date form of the Dorset trap the best and most effective all-round means of capture that exists, and until something equally practical and applicable can be invented we must be content to continue its employment, despite everything that is put forth as to the cruel manner of its working. How difficult it is to get away from the principle upon which it acts is shown by the persistent efforts fostered and made to produce something to serve a similar purpose, but with unvarying want of success. The Dorset trap, in its general features, is too well known to need any detailed description; but there are, of course, varied forms depending upon the class of workmanship put into them. It is necessary, however, to point out that it is impossible to produce good and trustworthy traps, even without finish, below a certain price, and that anything of the kind which may come under the description "cheap" is sure to prove troublesome, disappointing, and very dear in the ultimate result.

The main points of excellence in a Dorset trap intended for the capture of rabbits or furred and feathered vermin are found in a combination of lightness, strength, durability, and quick and certain action. These can only be assured when good workmanship is put into good material. In order that the prospective trapper may be able to judge of the merits of any traps submitted to him, I will describe succinctly the various parts, and point out at the same time in what respects they should chiefly show merit. The terms applied to the parts are those in most general use; but others obtain locally.

The frame of the trap should be straight and stiff, the cross-piece tightly and properly riveted to it; it should have plenty of substance in it, and the jaw-. pieces should be, in the one case, firmly and stiffly welded on; in the other be correctly turned up so that the jaws, whilst working easily, have no unnecessary play. The spring must be well tempered, strong and sufficiently pliant to be pressed down by the clasped hand to permit the jaws to fall into their natural open position when set. When set, the spring should act directly upon the jaws, the loop working free of the jaw-piece. When sprung, it should rise just to the level of the jaws, so as to hold them closed, without jamming heavily against their undersides. An average man should be able, by the grasp of a single hand, to depress the spring with a fair amount of ease; springs requiring a strong effort are too stiff; those which suffer depression too easily are too weak. As a rule, all springs are tested by the manufacturers before being sent out; but occasional failures through loss of temper may occur, in which case spare ones can be fitted. The spring should be well bolted to the frame, lie low at the bend, and not rise more than $1\frac{1}{2}$ inches from the level of the frame. The jaws should be strong and reasonably thick, the teeth, when the trap is sprung, leaving an appreciable margin of distance between them—say, one-

sixteenth of an inch. There are various patterns of
jaws, but those shown in the illustrations are the best
for general purposes. It must be borne in mind that
the jaws are intended to hold without cutting, and, if
possible, without breaking bone. The plate, treadle,
or trigger, I prefer to have of zinc, but under most
circumstances it serves equally well if it be of iron or
steel. The edges should be bevelled off, and the plate,
when the trap is set, lie nearly on a level, and in the
same plane with the jaws. It should work easily and
freely in its support, but have no lateral play. The
catch is fixed on the plate, and should be of brass, as
should be also the flap, although in most of the lower-
priced, but not necessarily bad, traps it is of iron.
Brass is to be preferred infinitely, however, and the
joints, if not the upright which holds the flap, should
be of this metal. The catches are, naturally, a very
important item, and when sent out they act, or should
act, perfectly, admitting of the trap to be set as "tickle"
or lightly as possible, or as firmly as may be desired.
With brass catches it is possible to so regulate the trap
that it will allow lighter animals, such as very young
rabbits, to pass over it with impunity, whilst three-
quarter or full grown ones would be taken. The chain
provided with a swivel is fixed to the frame of the trap
by an S-hook. All of these parts require careful examination, and, whilst being as light as possible, must
also be of sound material and good manufacture; the
same remarks apply to the rings at the chain-ends.
For general purposes the chain may be about the same
length as the trap; but in the case of small vermin
trapping the chains will exceed the length of the trap.

ORDINARY DORSET TRAP.

IMPROVED DORSET TRAP.

It is important that the swivels work easily and well,
and if more than ordinarily long chains have to be employed—as is sometimes the case—two swivels at corresponding distances from each extremity should be
employed.

The provision of stakes for the traps is always an
important matter, and one which should command
careful attention. It is not unusual with those employing Dorset and other traps to adapt any rough-and-
ready kind of stake for the purpose; but it is far better
to shape them out properly. After long experience, I
have found that for ordinary purposes the best stakes
are those shaped out of well-seasoned ash-wood. Cut
into lengths of 18in., it can then be split down to about
the right size—roughly, 2in. in diameter—and rounded
off, from about 1½in. from the top. It is not necessary
or advisable to make too neat a job of it; nor should the
stakes be gradually pointed off. Bring them down to
a size which will permit the ring being pushed to
within a couple of inches of its final position; then
gently hammer it down to there, and bring the other
end of the stake to a somewhat abrupt point. Made
and fastened on in this manner, these stakes will hold
in almost any ground, and will stand any amount of
hammering in without splitting. It is necessary to be
careful, however, that the portion which overlaps the
ring does not do so to too great extent, otherwise the
margin may split off when being hammered into the
ground. There are other forms of stakes, however, to
which reference will be made on a later occasion.

Before proceeding to a description of the several
varieties of the Dorset traps which at one time or

another recommend themselves for employment instead of those of the ordinary type, it may be necessary to mention that there are several grades of quality in the Dorset traps, the lower of which can be brought into use whilst at the same time being quite satisfactory. The chief disability attaching to them is that they do not last so long as those of higher grade. Then, again, they vary in size, this point being mainly determined by the width of the jaw; the longer the jaws, the more the cost. Certain sizes are most effective for certain purposes, and it is not always possible or wise to work with traps all of one size. There is also the difference in make between rabbit and vermin traps, the latter always having less material worked into them; so that, although the size denoted by width of jaw may, possibly, be the same, the traps of similar size may not be identical.

The variations of the Dorset trap are mainly of detail, rather than of form, as will be seen from the several illustrations which are given of the usual form of trap and of those differing from it in certain particulars. Some of these points of variance may appeal more to practised individual trappers than do others. So much is this the case that as the tyro in trapping develops into the expert, he will find himself working with one particular form of trap for general use with which he can do more good than with any other.

Beyond such details as size and weight- -and it must be remembered that traps of similar size are not by any means always of similar weight—the chief variations of the Dorset trap will be found in the jaws; whether they be ribbed or flat, close-fitting in the teeth, the shape of the latter, or without teeth at all. Generally speaking, flat-jawed traps are usually more easily worked upon grass-land, and ribbed ones where the soil is loose and sandy. The choice is dependent upon the question of covering the trap more than anything else, and it will be found that the respective forms lend themselves to the most effective work in this respect. Plain-jawed traps with no teeth at all serve best where the ground is very full of small stones which are calcu-

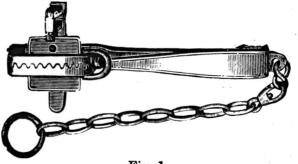

Fig. 1.
ORDINARY DORSET TRAP.

lated to get between the teeth of the jaws in such formed traps, and prevent them gripping when sprung.

The S hooks are not infrequently a source of anxiety and disappointment, in many instances losing their temper and pulling out, thus permitting the quarry to get away with the trap—a most unsatisfactory occurrence in every way, and one which, in addition to the mere material loss, leads to its dying in misery and torment. To prevent any such happening, the device of affixing the chain to the trap by a loop encircling the spring has been adopted, and is so much to be preferred that its use ought certainly to become general.

Another form of Dorset trap has the spring rivetted on to the under, instead of the upper, side of the stock or back-piece which permits of the employment of a well-bowed spring, which lies, however, very low when the trap is set. This is an important consideration, especially when working on certain classes of ground, notably thin soil and grass-land. Both of these improvements are shown in **Fig. 2.**

The firm of Henry Lane, Wednesfield, has lately

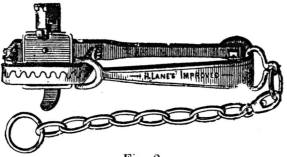

Fig. 2.

IMPROVED DORSET TRAP.

placed upon the market a Dorset trap in which the flat steel spring is replaced by one of drawn steel wire. As will be seen clearly from the illustration which I give of it, the motive power of the spring is centred in the coils, and, by reason of its form and the manner in which it is fixed, the spring, if broken or bent, can easily be removed and refitted without interfering with the jaws—a particularly meritorious feature, which is supplemented by another, a considerable reduction in the weight of the traps. These traps are only stocked in rabbit size, so far, but can be had in smaller or larger ones if the orders reach a sufficient quantity.

At Fig. 4 is shown another form of Dorset trap, with wire spring. In this case a single length of cold-drawn steel, forms the spring. These traps are very quick,

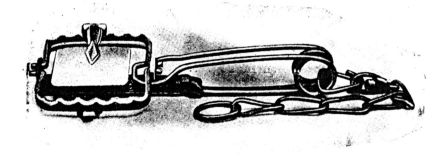

Fig. 3.

DORSET TRAP WITH WIRE SPRING.

hold very tightly, and are built to lie as flat as any I have handled. This is a manifest advantage in thin soils. They are very light, and withal durable. **Mr.**

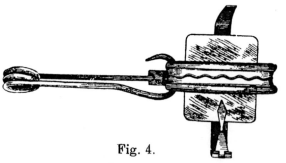

Fig. 4.

CRUICKSHANK'S DETACHABLE TRAP.

Cruickshank has introduced many small but important improvements into his traps, mainly designed to avoid sticking of the tongue and catch.

It has long been recognised that, while the **principle**

of the steel trap cannot be improved upon for practical
purposes, it possesses some disadvantages in the matter
of weight and difficulty of repair in case of breakage.
Many efforts have been made of late years to overcome
these disabilities with more or less success. The firm
of Henry Lane, Wednesfield, has recently patented an
entirely new form of the steel trap, in which all the old
points of excellence have been maintained, whilst an

Fig. 5.

THE COLLAPSIBLE TRAP, READY FOR USE.

entirely new system of construction is introduced by
which the weight is reduced by nearly one half, without
any loss of strength or effectiveness. In the new patent
the back piece is done away with, and the trap consists
of three separate portions, which are easily fitted together and form a stiff, compact trap. Reference to the
illustration shows how this is effected. The loop of the
chain is passed over the spring, which is compressed by
hand, or with the aid of a U-piece. The loop of the
spring is passed over the jaws by means of the slit and
the tongue inserted in the slot in the base of the trap.
The bridge is fitted by sliding into the groove in the

base, and is held in position by a finger-piece. It may be made a permanent fixture by using a split pin, which is also provided. The trap is then ready for use. Where necessary, a second spring can be similarly fitted. In its simple form for rabbits or vermin it is of less length and depth than the ordinary Dorset trap, more easily covered, and for the former purpose more adaptable for setting in rabbit holes. A dozen 4in. traps can be easily

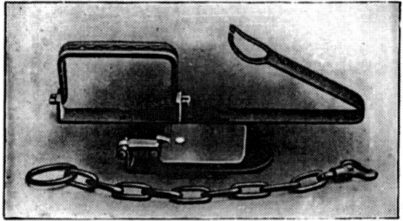

Fig. 5.

THE COLLAPSIBLE TRAP, DISMOUNTED.

carried in the pockets and be pieced together as required. When packed for transport these traps occupy one-fourth the space of the old type—a most important point as far as foreign and Colonial work is considered, where the cost and means of transport are far greater and much less respectively than in the homeland. In Henry Lane's new trap each and every part is interchangeable, so that by securing a supply of spare parts no trap need be put out of action pending return to a source of repairs.

CHAPTER II.

HUMANE TRAPS.

As I mentioned before, the principle of the Dorset steel trap cannot be improved upon for universal use or be substituted effectually by any other known at present. All attempts to embody the same principle in really humane traps of such general utility have proved, and appear bound to prove, failures. The well-intentioned efforts of all those who have encouraged the production or have produced humane traps have been frustrated either by ineffectiveness of the article evolved for practical working or by the expensiveness of its manufacture. The result is that, notwithstanding all the great diversity of traps in more or less everyday use, no actually humane trap of practical general utility exists. The nearest we can get to anything of the kind is to be found in modifications of the Dorset trap. The simplest manner of mitigating the breaking and lacerating effects of the jaws is to bind them over and over in between the teeth of the jaws with whipcord. The binding should not go over the teeth and reach to nearly flush with them. The more neatly and tightly it is done, the better, but it must be finished off at the turn of the jaws, and not be continued over the sides of them. Treated in this manner, strong-springed traps will hold rabbits and vermin for a reasonable length of time; but traps so treated require

more attention and frequent visiting than do others, as
many more will be found sprung, but empty, and, unless looked over every two or three hours, anything
caught is likely to work its way free and be lost.

A rather ingenious idea for rendering ordinary traps
"humane" as well as for use with specially constructed

Fig. 6.

MITCHELL'S HUMANE ADAPTOR.

ones, having plain jaws adapted for the purpose, is illustrated at Figs. 6 and 7. The humane device consists
of two pads of corrugated rubber fitted into containers of
sheet steel, which form the jaws of the trap. I have
experimented with a specially made and fitted trap,
which did all that was claimed for it in the way of

Fig. 7.

MITCHELL'S HUMANE TRAP.

breaking no bones, nor apparently causing any more
pain than was bearable by the animal or bird caught.

The adaptors containing the rubber can be applied to
ordinary tooth-jawed traps by filing the jaws to receive
them, or by taking them out and reversing them in their
sockets. The makers, Messrs. Wilkins and Wright,
Birmingham, claim that the rubber containers will out-

last the traps, which extended trial should confirm, and as the jaws do not in any way interfere with the setting and working of the traps, the invention is one which should commend itself to all those using steel traps to whom humane working is the first consideration.

Two forms of humane traps exist which may be employed—one with round jaws covered with rubber, the other flat-faced jaws, treated like a coarse rasp. I have

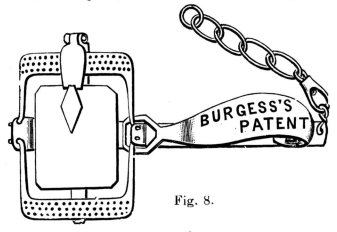

Fig. 8.

HUMANE TRAP WITH FLAT JAWS.

worked with both of these, mainly for winged vermin, for which they are quite effective; but they are less trustworthy for rabbits or furred vermin, possessing the same drawbacks in this respect as the ordinary traps whipped with cord. Carrion crows and big hawks are liable to tear off the rubber from the former if not speedily looked to after capture, and make their escape. These forms of traps do not differ as regards their manipulation from the ordinary Dorset trap, but, of course, they entail more trouble in the process of covering, the form of the jaws necessitating extra care in this respect.

There was another form of humane trap placed upon the market some years back, in which the jaws were absent and replaced by a bar of iron fixed at right angles on the extremity of the eye of the spring. This was held down in the ordinary manner by a flap and catch passing over the centre of the bar, which was released by the depression of the treadle. Over this was a hoop of steel wire, and the action of the trap was such that—it being set facing a hole—the rabbit coming out sprung the trap and had its neck broken by the bar flying up and jamming it against the steel hoop. It was a very good trap as far as theory went, but possessed little or no practical value.

Of course, there has been quite an alarming array of rabbit and vermin traps suggested and designed upon humane principles, with a view to the rewards offered for an effective instrument of the kind. Of humane traps distinct in form from the ordinary Dorset trap the most practical and effective is the one invented and patented by Mr. Frederic Sara, of Yelverton, Devon. It is designed mainly for rabbit-trapping, but the principle can be applied to the catching of furred vermin. As will be seen from the illustrations, the form of the trap differs from almost all others, as well as the principle upon which it acts, but the plate is retained as trigger, and it is employed and thrown in precisely the same manner as the ordinary Dorset trap, viz., by pressure of the rabbit's fore-feet. The plate or treadle, however, is divided and hinged, and folds over so as to admit of the passage upwards of the arms.

The trap is set precisely as would be a Dorset trap, covered in the same manner, and placed in suitable position in the run, at the holes or the scrapes. The rabbit

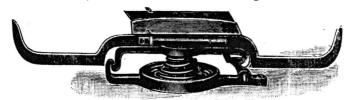

Trap set.

attempting to pass places one or both of its fore-feet on the plate or treadle, which is depressed, and releases the

Trap sprung.

arms, which fly up, encircling the rabbit's neck and breaking it at the same instant.

To my mind, this trap is the nearest solution of a practical nature of the problem of a really effective and humane trap which has been evolved so far. There is

no doubt that it will take rabbits as readily as the
Dorset trap, and the victim is killed simultaneously
without being mauled in the least. It possesses the
merit, moreover, that it is practically innocuous as far
as winged game, dogs, and foxes are concerned. Ex-

SARA'S PATENT HUMANE RABBIT TRAP.

periments made have proved that even a small terrier
can spring the trap without injury to itself, and, unless a pheasant actually pecks on the plate, and in one
position, it will not be caught. It is likely that to the
uninitiated the form of the trap appears peculiar, but
in practice it fulfils its purpose entirely. It weighs
about the same as a good-quality Dorset trap, and the
price is identical. It requires no more care, and entails no more trouble in setting. Altogether it is a
well thought-out and ingenious article, thoroughly well
fitted for use by practical men.

CHAPTER III.

TOOLS, ETC., FOR TRAPPING.

In addition to the actual traps, the trapper employing them requires one or two accessories which he would do well to carry with him, particularly when first commencing operations. Later on, when more expert, he will find that he can dispense with most of them at a pinch, although better work is, of course, accomplished with their aid than without them. The tools most usually employed are a trapper's hammer, a small sieve or riddle, and frequently a small bill-hook with a rather long handle, and, of course, a strong knife. A few spare S-hooks and rings for mending chains, a small bottle of neatsfoot or olive oil, a coil or two of fine copper wire, and a hank or two of whip-cord go to make up the rest of the impedimenta, and, with all these on hand, the trapper may be considered provided for most eventualities.

The trapper's hammer requires to be a handy and well-made tool, such as is shown in the adjoining illustration. They are very labour-saving, and when properly formed add greatly to the efficiency of the work done. The small sieve with folding handle is very portable, as it will go into the pocket; but a quite small wire one with bent wood sides is almost as handy. A straight-bladed knife with a large four or five inch blade and a small one besides is most suited for trapping work.

Of course, even the amateur requires a strong, rough get-up for the work in question, notably a coat with big pockets inside and out, and leather shoulder-pieces; and, as there is a good deal of kneeling and crawling about to be done at times, leather knee-guards and leggings are a necessity. There is one other point to be observed, namely, that at times, when watching the traps, or for possible quarry, sitting about on damp places is to be avoided if health is to be maintained, and a small square of waterproof carried in an inside pocket will always prove serviceable.

A close-fitting cap of the fore-and-aft description is the best headgear, and the big pockets afore-mentioned are the best receptacles for carrying tools and other impedimenta. Anything in the way of a bag or the like slung across the shoulders is an unending and unendurable nuisance.

It must be borne in mind that a trapper goes about his work easily and successfully, without leaving traces of his movements and operations wherever he has passed. It is rarely necessary to employ a bill-hook to clear away growth, and its indiscriminate use to make things easier is to be condemned. Now and again circumstances arise necessitating something of the kind, but the user of traps and snares will do best when he interferes least with the natural order of things where he places his wiles.

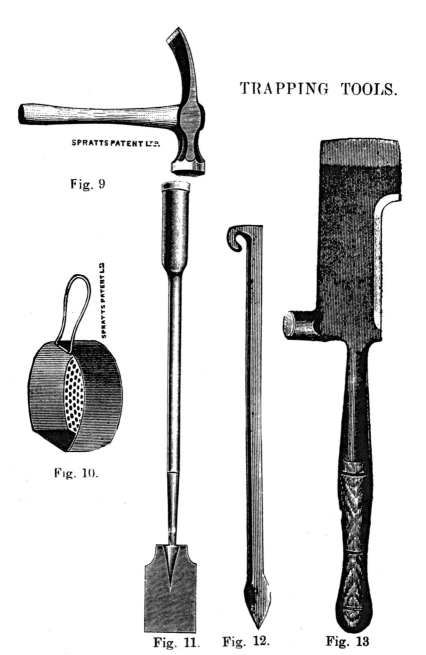

Fig. 9

Fig. 10.

Fig. 11.   Fig. 12.   Fig. 13

Fig. 9, Trapping Hammer; Fig. 10, Trapping Sieve; Fig. 11,
Trapping Spade; Fig. 12, Iron Stake; Fig. 13, Combined
Bill-hook, Hammer, and Spade

CHAPTER IV.

HOW TO SET THE DORSET TRAP.

As a rule, the person who handles Dorset and other traps for the first few times proves himself very awkward in dealing with them. The same may be said of a good many who are supposed to be thoroughly accustomed to them. The probable reason is that they have never overcome a natural nervousness in dealing with anything of the kind, and are fearsome of injuring themselves. It is, however, very easy and simple to become adept at handling them and to guard against anything, the proof of which may be found in the fact that in all the years and under all the circumstances that I have handled and employed traps of many forms, I have never once caused myself any injury worth the name.

To set an ordinary Dorset trap safely and easily, the following is the correct method :—Grasp the trap with the right hand across the spring, close down to the loop which encircles the jaws (but not close enough to pinch the loose skin of the hand), and depress it till the jaws fall apart; then, employing the left hand, and using the pad of the thumb and the second finger further to lever open the jaws, turn the flap over with the first finger, and with the third, under the plate or trigger, adjust the catch, and the trap is set. If the operation be not easily worked at first, use a trap with a very weak spring, or a quite small trap, until you can complete the setting in the manner named, without needing to observe what you are doing. It will be found that as confidence is gained in the manipulation of the trap, it is really quite easy to set hard-springed ones with very little trouble; and if such are being used, and prove too strong for easy handling in the manner described, additional power is gained by placing the trap across the knees—slightly bent for the purpose—the end of it resting upon the right, the jaws just over the left, and the hand grasping the spring between them. If it can be avoided, never kneel or place the foot upon the spring to depress it; and if, by physical weakness or infirmity, the trap cannot be set otherwise, a small screw-clamp or wrench may be employed to press down the spring and retain it in possession until the trap is fully set. When first set, the catch should fully fit in and hold the flap; but it can be regulated by depressing the plate so as to lie very "tickle," or hard, according to what is intended to be caught. This adjustment should be made before the trap is placed in position, as it is easier to judge the amount of "hold" there is on the trigger by holding the trap in a horizontal position on a level with the eyes than by attempting to regulate it when it is upon the ground.

. Under nearly all conditions it is necessary to cover the trap completely when set, and effectually hide it from the intended quarry. Upon the correct placing and covering of the trap depend the possibilities of success or failure in trapping. At first the tyro in trapping will find this part of the work beset with a good deal more trouble, and occupying much more time, than after he has had some practice and experience. Many difficulties accompany the proper covering of the traps at the outset, and it is fairly certain that the inexpert trapper will frequently find himself dissatisfied with his work. After a little, however, time and patience bring their reward, and he will find himself setting and covering his traps in quick time and to complete satisfaction.

Traps have to be set and hidden, of course, under many and varied conditions, but these can be brought under two main heads—traps placed upon grassy ground, and those upon bare soil. As a main guide to how to get to work, it will be necessary to take these two typical conditions and see how the trap is set under quite simple circumstances. A rabbit's run in a grass field may be chosen as the spot, in the first instance. Place the jaws of the trap in the position they would occupy when set at right angles to the direction of the run, and with the catch on the further side from where you are working. Then extend the chain to nearly its full length, leaving an inch or so play, and drive in the stake to its full length. The verdure should conceal the small portion of the stake protruding from the ground, and a pull should be made at the stake with the chain to make sure that it holds. The actual position of the trap having been decided upon, dig out with the hoe part of the hammer a square place to receive the jaws, and a small channel to fulfil the same purpose for the spring and back-piece. For the purpose of concealing the chain, a sort of flap covering can be similarly cut out. The bed hollowed out for receiving the jaws and spring must be so adjusted and flattened as to bring the upper surface of the former and the treadle with them slightly below the surface of the ground. The spring must lie also so that it is completely covered, and when the process of hiding the trap is finished, the surface above it must be left almost precisely as it was before operations were commenced.

Before commencing to cover up the trap, either a small flat stick or the blade of one's knife should be inserted over the jaw and under the treadle upon the side opposite the catch, to prevent the trap springing whilst being covered. The chain and spring are best dealt with first, and then the body of the trap. The aim in view in covering it over is to make endeavour to imitate as nearly as possible the exact appearance of the ground before it was disturbed to accommodate the trap. If the trap is placed upon grass-land with a short, thick covering—old pasture, in fact—then the best covering consists of fine, short grass, carefully plucked and closely scattered over the jaws and plate of the trap. Supporting the latter, the material may be pressed down closely and evenly, employing much or little, according to circumstances, and, if the surroundings warrant it, scatter a little fine, fresh mould over the short grass, as it will assist to keep the latter fresh and in position. Where the run passes through thick, heavy herbage, or coarse-growing grass, it will be necessary to vary the covering slightly, laying the grass, as far as possible, crossways with the jaws, so that they may throw it off when the trap is sprung; otherwise it may block them and prevent them working properly. Again, if the ground be mossy, the moss used for covering must be carefully pulled apart, and only the greener portions employed, as it fades and loses colour much more quickly than grass, which will retain its greenness and freshness for 24 hours or more.

From these few hints it will be seen that practically every different site chosen for the position of a trap upon grass land or ground covered with growth of any kind entails a variation in the manner of covering and the exercise of intelligence and care in the selection of the method of hiding the trap. It must be thoroughly covered, but the means adopted and the mode of doing this must not interfere with the working of it. Very little interposed between the jaws serves to permit the animal caught to liberate itself, whilst at the same time it is necessary to thoroughly hide the trap from view. It is in the correct and efficient assimilation of these two desiderata that the correct "tilling" of a trap upon grass-covered ground consists.

When and where traps have to be placed upon un-covered ground, such as bare soil of whatever nature, sandy, gravelly, or even stony, it is necessary, when preparing the hollowed-out bed for the trap's reception, to make it somewhat larger than when working upon grass-land, otherwise the earth or other soil running down at the sides will prevent an effective setting being made. Of course, the looser the soil in which one is working, the more margin of space must be afforded, because, although it is possible and easy enough to com-plete the setting and covering so as to make everything look all right at the moment, change of temperature, dew or rain, will cause the trap either to spring, or the covering to fall away and expose it to view.

The same end must be held in view when working traps in bare ground when setting and covering them, viz., that the fact of their being in position be hidden, and that the surface of the soil where they are set be made to exactly resemble what it was before being disturbed. As regards the main items in the operations for "tilling" the traps, there is nothing to add to the instructions previously given; but special care must be exercised in two directions. In the first instance, the presence of small stones, particularly where the jaws are hinged on to the frame, and also beneath the plate, must be carefully avoided. Then, again, where the soil is dry, fine, and very friable, it is very much disposed to run down under the plate and prevent its proper action when the quarry seeks to pass over it. The use of the sieve or riddle will prevent the former; but it must be remembered, when employing such, that it is easily possible to overdo the matter, and by eliminating all the little and big stones to make the position of the trap quite apparent, and the ground covering it so different from the rest of the run or form that an alarm is caused, and the intended capture scared away. Again, when working in very loose soil, it may be necessary to build up in between the jaws and plate with moss, lichen, or similar handy material, so as to prevent the soil running in under the trap, and also to provide something upon which the covering material may rest without interfering with the working of the trap. All of this entails delicate work upon the part of the trapper, which will cause him a good deal of trouble and anxiety at first; but he will soon get in the way of accomplishing all such little finessings.

It is also necessary when trapping upon bare ground to remember the effect of varying temperature upon the soil. Thus, traps set in damp or wet weather will become exposed when it turns dry, and will require overhauling to be effective; whilst rain, according to whether it be light or heavy, may cake the traps up so that they fail to act in many instances, wash them nearly clear of covering, or, perhaps, spring them right off. I used, when first trapping to any extent, to wonder what sprung my traps without leaving any clue to the cause, and in later years I have often been able to point out the cause to others. It is dew falling in the form of heavy drops from trees, hedge-growth, and the like overhead. As the dew condenses upon the leaves and boughs, it forms into very large drops, which, falling from a height, produce ample force to spring a trap, and when working under hedgerows or overhanging boughs from adjoining woods or plantations, the fact is extremely annoying. The leaves of brambles are particularly productive of this cause of sprung traps.

Wherever traps are placed, whether they effect their purpose or not, it will be necessary to overhaul them at repeated intervals, even to the extent of resetting them if necessary. It is also important, wherever a trap is sprung, either to reset it or to remove it, because it is really surprising to what an extent anything of the kind will affect the movements of intended quarry and baulk the effective result of the work. By overhauling I do not wish to imply continual interference with traps already set, but careful scrutiny of them from time to time, with the view to remedying any defects in their covering, etc., which may have arisen.

I have referred already cursorily to the necessity of
not disarranging the natural growth, etc., alongside
the runs, and so on, where traps are placed. If anything be so far in the way as to actually interfere with
the actual working of a trap, it may be removed, or its
position changed, but otherwise the process of "first
clearing away" should be studiously avoided. It may
be inconvenient not to do so, but it adds immensely to
the prospects of success to interfere with the surroundings as little as possible. It is difficult to exaggerate
the effect which such action has upon approaching
quarry, but the fact will soon make itself apparent to
the trapper as he gains in knowledge and experience.

Of course, as occasions arise and circumstances vary,
some modification of the manner of setting the Dorset
trap will have to come into use. In the first place, it
is always desirable to so place the trap that the catch
and flap are upon the site opposite to that from which
the intended victim is expected to approach. On the
other hand, in most instances traps set for rabbit
alongside hedgerows, hedges, burrows, and the like
usually find the most favourable positions with the contrary the case. Some people appear to think it makes
much difference; as a matter of fact, it is immaterial.
You will, however, find it is always easier to set the
trap and make a good job of it, with the plate towards
you. The most ineffective way of placing a trap is
with the spring in a line with the direction the quarry
is expected to pursue; whichever way it comes, the trap
is at a disadvantage. If it come over the spring, it is
likely to suddenly feel the metal beneath it and stop,
or abruptly change its path; if it comes the other way

on, it is not unlikely to place one foot upon the flap, and even, if it spring the trap, be thrown free of it by the upspringing jaws. When trapping on sloping ground, it is advisable, as a general rule, to place the trap with the flap side upon the lower level if the run traverses it in a vertical direction, but if in a horizontal one, the spring should lie below the jaws, and not above them.

Occasionally trouble occurs in obtaining a secure hold for the stake at a point distant from the trap the full length of the chain. In such cases it must be driven in nearer the trap, either beneath the jaws or to such a depth below the surface of the ground as to permit the chain being coiled up on the top of it in a small space made for the purpose. It must always be remembered that the full-sized Dorset trap for taking rabbits and anything larger is of a certain weight, and that the pull of the animal caught upon the stake is strong, and repeated for some length of time. No really satisfactory substitute for the wooden stake exists, and it must be made to hold properly and effectively in whatever position it is placed in reference to the position of the trap itself.

Before proceeding to deal with other forms of traps, a few points in connection with the general use of full-sized Dorset ones may be brought forward with advantage. In the first instance, the question as to how "tickle" traps should be set may be generally referred to. As a rule, the trapper errs on one side or the other; large traps too lightly set are likely to spring from unlooked-for causes, due to weather and temperature, whilst if set too hard, they are extremely liable .

to miss their mark, even if they are thrown by the quarry intended. Traps set in the open usually require to be set more "tickle" than those in woodlands, brakes, etc., and alongside hedges and banks. When the traps become rusted and dirty, soak them in paraffin to remove rust, and then wash them thoroughly in hot water with plenty of soda in it. Oil working parts with vegetable oil. Never employ mineral or animal oils or fats. Use the file very carefully and very lightly, and if traps require repair, send them to the makers for the purpose, and renew all S-hooks, chain parts, and stakes as soon as ever they exhibit signs of wear.

CHAPTER V.

ROUND AND SMALL STEEL TRAPS.

The employment for its main purpose of the round form or hawk trap has been largely diminished by reason of the Act which prohibits their use upon the tops of poles or posts, etc., in positions where they would be most effective. It must be conceded freely, however, that very great abuses attached to the careless and indiscriminate manner in which they were thus employed, the waste of inoffensive bird-life and the wholly unnecessary cruelty which they were permitted to inflict amounting to a grave scandal. There exist several ways of using these traps upon poles and trees which would render their working comparatively innocuous from the cruelty point of view; but it is very probable that in many widespread districts for every predatory bird taken whose habits were inimical to the interests of the game preserver, perhaps a dozen or more wholly harmless feathered creatures fell victims.

Round traps can still, however, be employed in a number of positions, both for ground and winged vermin, where the ordinary Dorset trap is inconvenient, if not unsuitable, and they must accordingly be included in the armoury of the trapper. The illustrations which are given of the several forms of round trap are, probably, sufficiently indicative of their general form and arrangement; but it may be necessary to add that they are built up on a circular base, supplemented with a cross-piece, which the spring in semi-circular form is rivetted to, and rises from the circular base. Otherwise the action of the traps is similar to the ordinary Dorset trap. The jaws may be plain or toothed, according to the quarry to be taken, and most manufacturers can supply these traps with the trigger action

Fig. 14.

ROUND OR HAWK TRAP, FLAT JAWS.

reversed, i.e., so that the treadle has to be raised in order to discharge the trap. It is frequently necessary when trapping to employ a bait fixed to the treadle in order to take the bird or animal by the neck. In such instances the creature is very prone to seize the bait, and, without in any way depressing the treadle, take it away by pulling. In such instances a trap with the ordinary catch would fail to act, whereas with the working arrangement reversed, it would do so. Traps fitted this way are usually termed "hugger" traps, and the principle is applied to the larger sizes for taking poaching dogs and cats.   It is hardly necessary to add that

Fig. 15.

ROUND OR HAWK TRAP, TOOTHED JAWS.

they kill their victim almost outright, and little or no noise is caused to draw attention or excite alarm.

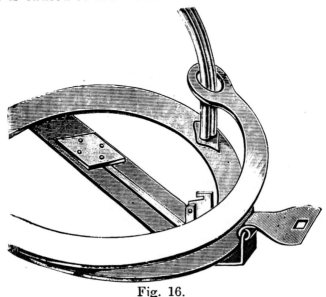

Fig. 16.

PULL-UP ACTION IN ROUND TRAP.

There exists a further form of trigger which permits of the trap being sprung either way by lifting or depressing. It is, however, somewhat uncertain in its action, being liable to discharge the trap very easily

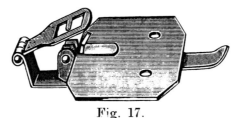

Fig. 17.

UP OR DOWN TRIGGER ACTION.

without the anticipated cause, and also requires neat and careful manipulation in the setting. For the benefit of those unacquainted with these two actions, I annex a sketch of them both.

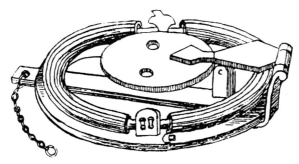

Fig. 18.

ROUND TRAP (HUMANE), RUBBER-COVERED JAWS.

These round traps can also be obtained with rubber-provided jaws, so as to avoid damage to the legs of any birds caught. When trapping for winged vermin, it is not infrequently the case that other birds whose capture is in no way desired become caught, and any provision which permits their being liberated without material hurt is very much to be desired. I have in practice always preferred to employ round traps with plain, blunt jaws, unless I could obtain toothed ones with the jaws so made and set as to prevent them actually striking together. Properly fashioned round traps meet these requirements, and when sprung, the jaws neither hit together nor do they leave too wide a space between. It must be remembered in connection with the trapping of winged vermin and birds in general that the jaws of a trap can encircle the legs without touching them at all, and still hold the captive fast, as the diameter of the foot is always from a half to twice as wide as that of the leg itself.

Continental trap manufacturers produce many modifications or elaborations of these round traps for employment in situations and under conditions which are not permissible in the British Isles, and I have fashioned traps for my own purpose of lighter and larger form in which wire and netting figured for the purpose of taking hawks, etc., alive.

SMALL STEEL VERMIN TRAPS.

Under this heading I propose to describe and figure three traps of American origin, and mainly employed in the States and Canada for taking musk-rats and such small deer. These traps, very light in construction, but strong and quick in action, I have employed over quite a number of years with great success—a result which has also followed in the case of those to whom I have recommended them. They are manufactured by Henry Lane, of Wednesfield, and are by no means expensive.

The first of them is a folding trap, the spring being capable of being folded round alongside the jaws, the trap being thus rendered more easily portable. This form of these traps is also the cheapest, the two latter requiring more care and time in manufacture. The second form, a single spring trap, is very compact and handy, with circular jaws. The arrangement of the

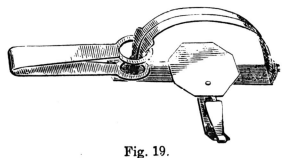

Fig. 19.

FOLDING VERMIN TRAP.

spring is notable, and reproduced in the third form a double spring trap with square jaws of larger and stronger size. These traps are so easily set, so light, and so portable, and, withal, so inexpensive, that they have everything to recommend them for employment wherever they can be brought into use. They can be worked with a light steel chain and iron stake, and be placed in a great number of effective positions where the ordinary Dorset traps are quite unsuitable for manipulation. They are used without teeth in the jaws, and, for all that, hold very securely. Chiefly adapted for small running vermin, I have found them equally effective for such winged marauders as magpies, jays, and the like. Their great merit becomes apparent

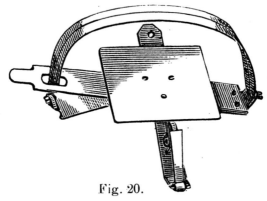

Fig. 20.

SINGLE-SPRING VERMIN TRAP.

when trapping has to be carried out upon grass-land or natural verdure, but notably in mossy and marshy

Fig. 21.

DOUBLE-SPRING VERMIN TRAP.

places; they are so easy of concealment and easily placed that anyone who has once handled them must find them indispensable to a thorough carrying out of his work

I have now described and figured those traps which may be regarded as the trapper's main instruments of warfare against nearly all the mischievous or predatory creatures whose capture is the ultimate aim of his machinations. These provide the basis, more or less, upon which all other of his work depends. For distinct pur-

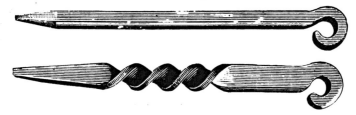

IRON STAKES FOR SMALL AND ROUND TRAPS.

poses and special quarry there are numbers of special traps which will come under consideration later. In the same way, snaring and the use of hingles, springes, and the like constitute a different department of the general subject, and require separate treatment. Our purpose must be now to learn how to set and employ those traps of which we have acquired knowledge.

CHAPTER VI.

HOW TO SET ROUND AND SMALL VERMIN TRAPS.

The round or hawk trap usually offers more difficulty to the tyro in trapping than do the Dorset traps. It is, as a matter of fact, more difficult to set, and more risks attend its handling; but, set in the following manner, its manipulation is handy and safe:—Grasp the trap across the spring and back-piece with the right hand, thumb uppermost, and depress the spring by using the pad of the thumb against the fingers beneath. This will release the jaws; then with the left hand, using the thumb, pull down the outer jàw, and, holding it firmly in position between thumb and fingers, control is obtained over the spring, and the right hand, being released, is employed to place the flap over the other jaw, the plate being raised and the catch fitted, thus completing the setting of the trap. Some of the larger makes of round traps are provided with two springs acting on each side of the jaws, but these are furnished —or should be—with a setting ring to the outer spring, which is first dealt with and held in position by the ring until the trap is finally set.

When employing round traps they are almost invariably placed in positions where the form of the Dorset trap prevents its use with practical success. In great numbers of cases the trap will be placed on a ledge, a tree stump, bough, and such-like unhandy

spots, and as the almost inevitable outcome of its being
sprung will be its fall or displacement, a different form
of chain is usually necessary to secure effectiveness in
the working of the trap. To this end a certain number
of the round traps in use should be fitted with from
2ft. to 3ft. lengths of small steel chain into which one
or two easily working swivels have been fixed. Further, it will very frequently be found that with these
long chains—and, in fact, with round traps in general
—the stake can be dispensed with in favour of some
form of staple employed to attach the end to tree stems,
boughs, posts, or rails. The ordinary staple to drive
in is not a very practical means for the purpose, and
suitable ones to screw in should be obtained, those with
a deeply-cut worm and sharp point being of the necessary description.

Those who find it obligatory to employ a considerable
number of round traps for taking winged vermin and
other birds for whose capture round traps are found
mainly suitable would do well to have a certain proportion of them specially made, in which the plate gives
place to a kind of forked treadle with two sharpened
points, upon which a small piece of tree-twig can be
fixed so as to offer a favourable perching-place. The
larger sizes of round trap, fitted with light, but sharp,
springs, are the best for the purpose; but it should be
borne in mind that in the case of the smaller ones the
trap must catch the victim by the legs, in the other by
the body, unless a bait takes the place of the perching
twig, when, according to the nature of the bird, it will
be taken by the legs or by the neck.

The actual setting of the round trap, to make it tho-

roughly effective, entails less work, but greater nicety
of manipulation, than the Dorset trap. Now that its
employment is restricted, the practice of using it without covering at all is reduced to very confined limits,
and as its employment in this manner upon poles, etc.,
involved an enormous waste of bird-life other than that
of predatory ones inimical to the game preserver, this is
a subject rather for congratulation than regret. In
almost all cases the hawk trap, when requiring covering to be effective, will be positioned amongst verdure
of some kind into the composition of which moss enters
more or less, and for the purpose of concealing the trap
nothing is more adaptable, properly employed. If
upon the ground, the place for it will require hollowing
out, and if set upon tree stumps or boughs, or upon
heavily moss-covered stones, etc., the growth will have
to be removed accordingly. The round trap is much
more liable to become jammed by small sticks and
stones getting in between the working parts than the
ordinary form of trap, notably between the jaws and
beneath the treadle. It is necessary, therefore, when
"packing" the trap, to see that there is nothing likely
to get in the way and prevent true working. To this
end, the jaws should not have anything crossing them,
and when the trap is covered, they should be practically free of any possible obstruction. The covering of
the treadle, etc., will depend upon the manner in which
the trap is being employed. Speaking generally, however, the best form of covering is that resembling in
the closest manner the surface of the ground which the
trap occupies; but it must always be remembered, in
view of the habits of predatory birds in general, that

they rarely place their feet or claws in a depression,
however small, and that any slight elevation offering
the merest means of a slight grasp by the retracted
claws or talons always commands preference as a foothold.   It is, therefore, better to err in having the covering of the plate or treadle above the level of the jaws
than below it.   To the more immediate details accom-
panying the use of the round trap I shall devote further
attention when treating of the capture of winged vermin and similar feathered quarry.

In expert hands there are no more easily set and
handled traps than the light steel ones illustrated at
figures 19, 20, and 21.   In none of them are the springs
very powerful, although amply strong for their purpose.   In each case, however, the actual setting of the
traps is effected very much as in the case of the round
trap, the transfer of the work from one hand to another
as the trap is opened being the key of the matter, the
point to be observed being that the jaws are automatically held open and the spring depressed by the outer
one, whilst flap and catch are manipulated into position.

These traps are best worked with rather long, light
chains and either iron stakes, as mentioned, or screw
staples for attachment to trees, railings, etc.   These
traps are of so light and unobtrusive construction that
they may be worked successfully with but very little
covering at all, and, except under special circumstances (where, for instance, a particularly wary customer has to be circumvented), I have rarely gone to
the trouble of packing them as one must the ordinary
descriptions of traps, a reasonably careful concealment
of plate and springs being sufficient for most purposes.

They can be placed in working position in all sorts of odd runs, nooks, and crannies where any other kind of trap is entirely out of the question, so that the variations in the manner in which they may be set extend to too large a category to be individually described. It may, however, serve a useful purpose to point out that they may be set amongst long grass and other verdure without further concealment than is naturally afforded; placed upon small runs on the sides and slopes of hedgerows where vermin may pass with but very little means of concealment, and upon rocks, old timber, palings, and such-like, where the merest of what may be termed parasitical verdure affords means of covering their whereabouts. They are particularly easily set, and concealed in mossy, marshy ground where heavier traps are entirely out of the question.

It will have been observed that these little traps are made without teeth to the jaws; but they hold firmly and securely without any such addition, and may be relied upon thoroughly for employment under any of the circumstances for which their use is recommended.

CHAPTER VII.

RABBIT TRAPPING.

In connection with this portion of the subject it is necessary, before dealing with the practical part of it, to glance for a moment at the limitations which the law places upon the use of spring traps for taking rabbits. The Ground Game Act limits the "occupier," as distinct from the owner, to their employment "in rabbit holes," which those who propound the law as formulated by Parliament for the mystification of the public take to mean "within the limits of the entrance to a rabbit burrow." The object of this limitation, when secured by the opponents of the Bill in its original form, was to prevent injury to and destruction of feathered game and —incidentally—sporting dogs. As a matter of fact, this limitation has reduced the use of the Dorset trap by occupiers to the smallest possible scope and the least effective manner. Whether the "occupier" always observes the strict letter of the law is doubtful and beside the question; but inasmuch as he is supposed so to do, I will in the first place deal with the trapping of rabbits as by the "occupier" under the Ground Game Act as being a mode of working quite apart from any other such as the actual owner of any land preserving it himself is entitled to permit his keeper to employ.

It is further to be presumed that the occupier trapping for rabbits does so to protect his crops from their

ravages; consequently, he will be doing so at such
seasons as will render his efforts most effective, viz.,
the spring and early summer. I have remarked, however, that the occupier appears to prefer rabbits to
crops, and does most of his "keeping down" during the
later and winter months, when dog and gun, ferrets and
nets, appeal more strongly to him as the best means of
doing it.

During the springtime rabbits will require killing
down round the growing corn and the new pastures,
clover and the like; the old pastures can take care of
themselves as far as rabbits are concerned. It is at
this season that rabbits show most fresh workings.
They are opening up their burrows again after the
winter inactivity, and with the breeding season commencing, they certainly make their presence upon the
farm very apparent and confessedly destructive. Several different kinds of workings will make their presence
known. Does in kindle, in the first place, start all sorts
of false burrows, and it is generally the most unlikely-
looking of them to the unpractised eye which is actually
the kindling burrow. Obviously, if does have to be
killed off at this season, it is better to take them before
than after the young are born. As a matter of fact,
this is the easier task, because few does make a kindling
burrow at all suitable for trapping in, and even then
they are difficult to take, as their instinctive scenting
of danger is extremely acute. Rabbits working in the
banks and hedgerows, and in burrows in woodlands,
brakes, and the like adjoining agricultural land, offer
the best opportunities for the employment of traps; but
I must admit that, except on the score of want of

time, there is little to warrant the use of them thus early in the season. Still, there are occasions and circumstances which make this a necessity at times, and on the score of thoroughness they must not be overlooked.

When the rabbits commence to open up their burrows afresh it is little use trapping for them until the throwing out of earth comes to an end. Once this is the case at a hole where working has been proceeding, evidence of the passing in and out of the rabbit or rabbits over the freshly moved earth will be apparent, and traps may be put down. It is necessary to select the holes in which to trap with discrimination, for there will be, probably, only one in every three or four which is fitted for the purpose, and not a large proportion of these in which a trap can be placed in workmanlike manner.

Choose the lower holes to which a well-marked and well-worked run leads, holes where the entrance is fairly high and sufficiently wide, and where there is a level space just within the run where the trap can be placed upon the "tread" of the rabbit. As is known, rabbits proceed by a succession of sharp leaps which may be designated by dots and dashes; the dots are those portions of the run where it does not place its feet, the dashes where it does do so. This action is shown more clearly at Figure 22. The treads or patches are about nine inches apart, and are observed by all but the quite immature rabbits when passing over a run, and the trap must be placed as stated. Slowly moving rabbits will be caught by the forelegs if the trap be placed in the centre of the patch, or, maybe,

E

by the hind legs if moving very fast, the tread of the
former being so extremely light and quick in the latter
instance as either not to spring the trap or to leave it
before the jaws rise, or, possibly, the two circumstances
combine to cause the animal to be taken by the hind
legs.   It is not very exceptional for a rabbit to be taken
by two legs, either both fore or one fore and one hind
legs, when trapping in the burrows.

Having determined upon a hole within which to set
the trap, 3in., 3½in., or 4in. jaws, as the case may be—

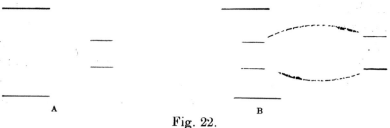

Fig. 22.

FOOTPRINTS OF RABBIT.

A, at starting; B, leap completed.

you will require a selection of sizes when working in
this manner--place the trap, unset, in its prospective
position to see if the jaws will work within the height
of the hole; then set it and try it for width.   There
must be ample margin without breaking down the sides
or roof of the hole.   Wherever practically possible, the
trap should be set with the spring at right angles or
obliquely to the direction of the burrow, because, if the
spring be worked in the line of it, a rabbit seeking to
enter is almost sure to discover the fact, stop dead, and
return in its tracks.   You will have to place the trap
with the plate towards the outside, and the space for its

reception must be scooped out First, however, lay the
trap in position, extend the chain, and drive in the
stake. Then hollow out the square space for the jaw,
dig out that for the spring, and equally for hiding the
chain. Now set the trap, adjust the tongue to the
catch, so that it a little more than holds, and place it
in position. A small stick or the blade of your knife
inserted over the jaw and under the plate will sustain
the latter without raising it. If you raise it, you re-
duce the "tickleness" of the setting. The soil which
has been removed to make the hollow within which the
jaws lie should be formed up round the outside of them
in little ridges, and should serve for covering; but, if
necessary, may be supplemented with other obtained
from the workings of the burrows, but not from any
portion over which the rabbits may pass. Using the
knife or small stick, and eliminating any stones, or
causing them to fall where they will not interfere with
the working of the trap, the loose soil should be carefully worked over flap or tongue, plate, etc., so as just
to cover it, and also to fill up all the interstices between
the working parts of the trap, but not in such manner as
to prevent the depression of the plate by the animal
placing its feet upon it. If the soil be very dry and
sandy, and inclined to run, you must build up between
the plate, jaws, etc., with moss or some material suitable, so that the free and quick working of the trap is
in no way interfered with. The covering must be completed so as to make it resemble the surface before any
disturbance of the soil took place. Pat it down carefully, whilst sustaining the plate, if it be a well-worked
burrow, or leave it rough if only slightly so. The

covering of the spring and chain must be similarly
effected so as to exhibit as little sign of disturbance as
possible.

Occasions may arise when it may be quite impossible
to find a suitable position for the trap without placing
the spring in the same line as the entrance into the
burrow. When such is the case, endeavour must be
made to bury the spring as deeply as possible without
affecting the correct setting of the jaws, otherwise, as
before stated, any rabbit seeking to enter the burrow
will feel it and return in its tracks. As a rule, however, traps so set will take rabbits as they seek to leave
their burrows, particularly if they be set at such time of
day when the rabbits have just gone in from feeding.

Opportunities for trapping rabbits at the burrows
under the conditions which the Ground Game Act pre-
scribes are really very limited, and severely handicap
the trapper in the exercise of his craft. As a rule, he
has to make up for restricted conditions by putting
down a far greater number of traps than would otherwise be necessary, and so making it almost impossible
for the rabbits to leave their burrows without encoun-
tering a trap. This is, of course, not trapping proper,
but there is no other way out of it.

The trapping of wild rabbits, without reference to any
limitations which the Ground Game Act may place upon
the operations of the trapper, is a far more extensive
matter, and provides so many opportunities for working
traps under such varying conditions than in dealing
with it, the information and instruction given serve
very well for the basis upon which other forms of trapping for other furred and feathered quarry may be

built up. A successful rabbit trapper is invariably a
good vermin catcher, and to be the former almost as
close and keen powers of observation are necessary as
with the latter, as well as a certain amount of delicacy
of handling of the traps, and skill in placing them.

Generally speaking, where rabbits are trapped to any
extent upon warrens, waste-lands, and other such
ground where "conies most do congregate," the regular season for the work commences usually early in
October, but sometimes even earlier. We have regarded the legitimate season for rabbit-trapping, however, as extending from the first week of that month
onwards through the autumn and winter, until such
time as the bulk of them are practically cleared off.
Snaring sometimes runs hand in hand with trapping,
but we must leave the former method of taking rabbits
for separate consideration at a later date; but before
commencing to trap or snare, or both, the ground
should be gone over thoroughly, and a comprehensive
knowledge of the possibilities it offers be acquired. It
is necessary to devote as much attention to those portions of the ground where the rabbits are, apparently,
less plentiful as where they appear most numerous, because it is not infrequently the case that comparatively
or actually more quarry will be taken at the first trapping upon the former description of ground than upon
the latter. A general scheme of operations—a plan of
campaign, in fact, should then be decided upon, which
shall have for its aim a regular compassing of the
ground upon such lines as will, whilst securing a large
and regular bag, not drive the rabbits from the open
ground to the woods and other coverts. To this end all

trapping within the limits of the woods, plantations, and other lands to which the rabbits betake themselves in winter should be relegated to the last portion of the trapping season.

Upon every manor where rabbits exist there will be some portions which they more greatly affect than others, and it should be the aim of the trapper to pick up the bulk of them where they are most plentiful at the start and then work steadily through the more scattered portions of the stock. No good purpose is served by making a half-hearted onslaught upon the rabbits where most numerous, otherwise the result is only to cause them to spread about and seek fresh quarters, thus adding to the trouble and cost of taking them. Of course, a certain area of the ground must be dealt with at a time, and my experience is that one man working over fairly favourable ground will find five dozen traps about as many as he can employ effectually and make full use of. It is, however, quite feasible to have more than this number in work, particularly if one's whole time be given up to it, and there is help to be obtained in dealing with the caught rabbits preparing and sending them to market. The traps will have to be supplemented in places by snares, and some netting and ferreting may also have to be done, but the quantity named of five dozen traps all in effective working order will be found to be just about as few or as many as one man can efficiently employ. Any increase of hands means a comparatively larger number of traps to be worked; thus two men should easily work and control twelve to fifteen dozen traps, and so on.

I shall, however, deal with rabbit trapping as if there

were only one person employed in the work, and that the number of traps be as stated. To properly utilise them the ground must be gone over first; there will be parts where the traps must be laid thinly, others where the difficulty will be to select the site from a superabundance of favourable ones. Having decided upon the extent of ground to be dealt with first, the trapper will start off with a third or half of his whole supply of traps, and, selecting a sufficient portion of his ground, proceed to dispose the traps in such places as he considers likely to produce the best results. Each trap should not be set individually at the site chosen, and then another, and another, and so on; but the ground should be properly quartered, as it were, and so provisioned with traps as to thoroughly include all possible avenues with certain limits. Do not trap at doubtful places, and do not be sparing of traps where the prospects appear favourable. Further, do not seek to find difficulties by placing traps in impossible positions, and always bear in mind the fact that where the setting can be made most satisfactorily in the way of placing, covering, etc., the best opportunities for success exist. A wholesome combination of snares and traps is sometimes of more service than a superfluity of either. Having finally surveyed the disposition of the traps and seen that the ground is effectually provisioned with them, the trapper can then proceed to set them in the manner already described, taking mental note of where each one is placed and where his work commences and ends.

As far as the trapping alongside hedgerows and at open burrows is concerned, there is little to be said as regards the way in which the traps should be placed,

but it will soon become evident to the trapper that under
certain circumstances the rabbits may be expected to
come out warily on one side of a bank or hedgerow, and
at others on the reverse side. Direction of the wind,
time of the day, etc., influence them in these respects,
and it is necessary to observe carefully and act accordingly. During the early portion of the season, traps
placed alongside woodlands, brakes, spinneys, or the
like should be placed to take the rabbits coming from
within, or which may be located in the hedgerow or
bank. There are generally a number of play-holes outside the covert which are only occasionally resorted to by
the rabbits, and which afford little scope for the trapper,
as the markings they show are in no way an indication
of the rabbits which use them. The runs leading outwards into the field, the scrapes which the rabbits form
some distance out from the boundaries, and actually
worked and tenanted burrows in the fields provide the
most fruitful sources of captures.

When rabbit trapping under these circumstances, endeavour should be made to make the captures as the rabbits work outwards, and not as they return to their
burrows. This is important, because the manner of
movement of the rabbits in the first instance is much
more favourable to the trapper than in the second, and
the traps must be so placed in the runs as to secure these
results. I have already explained the nature of a rabbit's run, and how and where it places its feet, so that it
is easy for the trapper to exercise his discrimination in
placing his traps and lay out to take his quarry precisely
as he desires to do.

I am afraid it would be rather unprofitable to endeavour to describe which runs and which workings are the really worked ones, and which have been more or less abandoned. To the unpractised eye, many of both appear to be "just the places" to utilise, whereas the opposite is the case. As a slight guide, it may be mentioned that in pastures and grass-fields where the droppings along the runs are dry and faded, there is little or no use made of them. The same may be said of those where new growth is showing untrampled between the old verdure. Runs over bare ground, where small growth of grass, weeds, etc., is showing in the tracks of the rabbits are also little worked, or not at all. Newly-made and somewhat ill-defined runs are more productive than old, clean-cut ones. Newly-worked burrows, where the earth thrown out is not worked down at all, are less productive, too, than old ones, where the entrances, etc., look clean and fresh, not old and dry. Rabbits' fleck in and about a hole shows free use and many users. Look for the same evidence on briar, thorn, and thistle overhanging or bordering hedgerow runs, and those leading more or less parallel to the hedges. Newly bitten-off and exposed roots exposed at the scrapes are proof that the rabbits will come again.

The time of day when traps must be set depends, of course, upon circumstances When first commencing to trap, or when breaking new ground, a start should be made in the morning as early as is reasonably possible. Thus, in the regular season, a couple of hours after sunrise—say about eight o'clock—a start may be made. Following the instructions for disposing of them, it will be found that the bulk of the forenoon will be consumed in placing and setting all, or nearly all, of

five dozen traps. If not finished up then, the balance
can be put down in the early afternoon. At other
periods of the year, when trapping is undertaken to preserve the crops from depredations, I have found that
the most productive time to set or reset the traps is
during the hour of first dawn ; but, with this exception,
the ordinary hours for working remain much the same.
In the case of commencing operations, those traps put
down and set in the early morning commence taking
rabbits in the afternoon, except, of course, in the case
of casual ones which may come out between times.
Following the afternoon catch, which will occur from
about two hours before sunset, there will come the night
catch subsequent to nightfall, and continuing to nine
or ten o'clock. There will be also an early morning
one of small importance, as a rule, about dawn. It
must, however, be remembered that the movements of
rabbits are very largely dependent upon influences of
weather, present and prospective, and it will become
incumbent upon the trapper to employ his powers of
observation at varying seasons and under varying circumstances, so as to acquaint himself with those influences and shape his actions accordingly.

It follows, therefore, from the foregoing that, having
his traps prepared, the trapper will have to make his
rounds at such times as will interfere least with the
movement of the rabbits, and when his traps should
provide the largest quantity of captures. Under ordinary circumstances, the first will fall, in the South
of England, or at a corresponding time in other districts, between half-past three and five, when the trapper will make his round, remove all rabbits caught, and

reset all traps sprung. Discretion must be employed in regard to moving any of the traps to fresh positions when the workings of the caught rabbit to escape have seriously interfered with or spoilt the sites chosen for them. In about four hours' time—say, between seven and eight—a second round must be undertaken, if the weather and circumstances warrant, which they will do in most cases. Personally, whatever the weather, I have never failed to take this round, and always insisted upon employees doing the same. Given an average bright, clear night, moonlit or starlit, a lantern is hardly necessary, but may be carried in case of requirement. Upon dark nights it is more or less a necessity. The best form of lantern is a small square one, burning colza oil, and having a single forward light, and with the handle at the top. It is advisable to employ the lantern as little as possible, and not flash it about indiscriminately as you go on your way.

Wherever advisable, sprung traps should be set again, and as soon as day has fairly broken, the trapper should again be out to take up any further catches.

How often to reset, and how long to persevere with, the traps upon a certain beat are matters which the trapper must decide for himself. He ought to be able to judge fairly accurately when he has cleared out the bulk of the rabbits from a certain extent of ground. A point will be reached when, if there be any more remaining in the burrows, he will not find it worth while to persevere at the moment, as the rabbits become so scared they will starve themselves for days on end sooner than come out to meet the fate which they have learned is likely to be in store for them. Then it is that, as soon as the range of traps proves profitable no longer, they should be taken up, carefully overhauled as to stakes, chains, etc., and transferred to another field of operations. As a rule it is best, where the circumstances permit it, to move the traps in successive batches, so that there is a little overlapping as far as the ground covered is concerned; whilst endeavour should be made, as far as possible, to work the traps round on the outer portions of the manor, and gradually centre them upon one or more given points.

Three causes for ineffectual working of the traps will crop up from time to time, excessive dryness affecting grass-covered ones, and rain and frost interfering with others. The former is met by extra attention to the traps, but the latter cause "sticking" or jambing of the traps in the working parts of any traps not of the very best working character. Both the tongue or flap and the plate hinge are liable to do this. Rain drives fine earth and sand into the interstices, and thus the parts "stick," or else frost freezes them, and they remain stiff and immobile. The reason is usually the lack of lateral movement in these working parts—there is not enough "play" in them. Whenever traps stick, then, in this manner, they must be looked to, and the indirect cause remedied. As regards rain and sand working in, it is, of course, impossible to entirely provide against; but one of our chief trap manufacturers is engaged in perfecting an arrangement which will permit of the freest lateral movement in these working parts, and at the same time exclude rain and sand or fine earth.

Rain and frost are two bugbears of the rabbit trapper,

adding very largely to the work attaching to the effective working of the traps. The only way to meet the difficulties is by assiduous attention to the traps, resetting and trying them, and seeing that the particular points to which I have directed attention are free of moisture and particles of foreign matter. All of these matters to which I have referred may influence the trapper in the scheme he adopts for moving his engines, because the weather may exert considerable influence upon this portion of the business; but it will be found generally the case that the same description of weather which compels a change of venue in the traps will influence the rabbits in the direction in which they are changed.

A word as to the manner of handling the rabbits when caught may serve to bring us to the end of this portion of the subject. When a rabbit is in a trap, it will generally lie low at the moment of your approach, and should then be seized, released, and killed as speedily as possible, so as to prevent the animal crying out, if possible. To do this effectually, place the foot firmly, but gently, upon the spring of the trap, and grasp the rabbit so as to place its hind legs in your one hand and its head in the other, ready for killing. A light tarpaulin bag is the best carrier for the rabbits taken. Of course, in wet weather it is practically impossible to keep the captures dry, but the tarpaulin bags do not increase the wetness, as do canvas ones. Rabbits should be cleanly paunched, hamstrung, and hung up in well-assorted couples ready for marketing.

CHAPTER VIII.

TRAPPING GROUND VERMIN.

Before going into the precise details which govern the trapping of ground vermin, it is necessary to refer to some general points which apply in regard to the traps employed, and the manner of using them. I have provided, for the most part, illustrations of the traps of all-round application, but at a later stage I shall describe a number of special ones devised for special conditions not met by the ordinary class of trap, but which, obviously, it would be hardly practical to deal with until we have the chief principles of vermin catching explained.

The ground vermin with which it will be necessary to deal first comprise the polecat, stoat, weasel, and common rat. A larger class of ground vermin includes wild cats, poaching cats, foxes (in certain countries), and poaching dogs. Of the former class the polecat is becoming less numerous yearly, and its habitat more restricted. Stoats and weasels do not appear to diminish seriously in numbers, despite the continuous onslaught upon their ranks, and rats were, probably, never so numerous as nowadays.

Speaking generally, a large trap is more effective than a small one, but for small quarry, such as the before-named species of vermin, it is very frequently necessary to employ smaller traps than one would otherwise do, owing to the exigencies of the circumstances under which trapping is being carried on. Small run traps of the Dorset pattern and others such as have been figured and described are applicable in a hundred places where larger ones would be useless; whereas, wherever the trapping is but little incommoded by the surroundings, I should always prefer a 3in., 3½in., or even 4in. trap for small vermin. The traps can be set every bit as ticklishly as smaller ones, and the victim is usually killed at time of taking, which is a matter for satisfaction, and frequently relieves the vermin-trapper of much trap-visiting which would otherwise be necessary. Then, again, the smaller run traps are not, as a rule, to be depended upon for effective working over a lengthened period without resetting.

Of course, the polecat, where in evidence, requires à fairly large trap, in any case, to hold it but quite a small one will suffice for stoats or weasels. Then, again, mature rats certainly entail the use of fair-sized traps to hold them successfully. It will be seen, therefore, that, even in the case of the smaller ground vermin, it is preferable to work with moderate-sized traps, wherever practicable.

The question of the covering up or complete hiding of the traps when employed on vermin-catching is rather a peculiar one and difficult to explain to the tyro. The general rule is that, the better a trap is concealed, the more effective it is in use. And yet there arise very frequently circumstances when careful covering is time and trouble misspent. Notably does this occur at times when trapping stoats and weasels; but with the polecat it is also the case. In connection with rats,

however, I am absolutely convinced that it is only by
the closest and cleverest of work that the trapper can
confidently grapple with these pests. Anything in the
way of careless or slipshod work is hopeless, as far as
serious or effective results are concerned.

Ground Vermin : The Polecat.

The smaller ground vermin have many characteristics in common, such as a large amount of natural cunning, bloodthirstiness, and pluck in defending themselves; but they each possess certain traits by which
they differ in habit from one another.

Wherever the polecat still exists, it remains the most
rapacious, as well as the largest, although least plentiful, of the small ground vermin. It is a deadly enemy
to game, notably winged game, and equally destructive
to poultry of every kind when and wherever chance
offers. A polecat is quite capable, and if unchecked
will repeatedly accomplish the task, of killing as much
game in one night as it could consume in a month. It
stalks and creeps upon its victims, bites quickly into the
brain, attacks the jugular vein, and sucks the life-blood
from it. If it consumes any of the flesh, it will commence where the neck issues from the breast bones,
tearing the flesh from the upper parts of these portions
of the victim, feathered or furred. It hunts for the
most part by night, from dusk to dawn, but hares it
will steal upon by day at times, whilst it will also attack
rabbits in their burrows. A slightly redeeming feature
is that the polecat destroys a good many rats from time
to time, when these latter vermin become plentiful.

It is impossible to enter into any detailed description of the polecat and its habits beyond the limits absolutely necessary for the purpose of the trapper. To this end it may be stated that polecats vary much in fur and colouring, according to the time of year; that they are more inclined to pursue a sequestered existence than a gregarious one; that the breeding-place is most frequently placed in a rabbit burrow in sandy soil, otherwise the animal will scoop out a lair for itself or choose a spot amongst the rocks or heaps of large stones. The young—four to six—are produced in May or June, and its usual haunts are not chosen in the neighbourhood where its breeding place is situated.

If I describe succinctly in turn the chiefly favoured haunts of the several species of ground vermin, it will suffice to give the prospective trapper such insight into the proper situations for placing his traps as will serve for the basis of his work. It is, obviously, out of the question to specialise each and every possibly successful site for a trap, and the trapper must, by observation and study of the habits of his quarry, come to a proper discrimination in these matters.

Speaking generally, any rough and broken ground, closely wooded or covered with brake, provides the main haunts of the polecat. It may take the form of small, dark fir-woods; low, thick brake, where blackthorn, briar, and bracken supply the growth; and each and all of those odd bits of rough covert and spinney which occur almost invariably upon every sporting estate. These, amongst them, provide the main characteristics of the haunts of the polecat, which are determined also

F

frequently by the presence of a stream or burn bordering or threading their limits. The polecat, however, has few or no defined regular runs or paths such as for the most part are affected by the stoat and weasel, and is as likely to lay off in one direction as another when leaving its lair. It possesses, however, the marked characteristic of all the weasels, of running the hedgerows or fences, working or playing about gates and gaps, and is a good and frequent climber of the larger specimens of the deciduous trees.

As a rule, the polecat either drags or carries away its victims to its nest or lair, or else to some other place of concealment; but rabbits it usually leaves dead a foot or so within the burrow where they may have been killed; so that evidence of depredations by this vermin is usually somewhat meagre. Sometimes, however, they will maul their victims about considerably, as if in wanton lust of the pleasure of killing. The fœtid odour, too, is left upon the victim, so that it is easy to verify the cause of its death. For the most part, despite the facts just mentioned, it is chiefly by the evidence left of their depredations that the presence of polecats is made manifest, although by close notice and watching it is possible even to view the "varmints" or make sure otherwise of their comings and goings. If a polecat hide up or leave its victim, it is sure to return to it, and as it is easily possible to know from the manner of killing what vermin has done the mischief, traps can be placed accordingly, employing the bird or animal killed as the bait. It is best to leave the latter in the place and position found, but, at the same time, to take the precaution to peg it down securely, as by reason of

its size and strength the polecat makes little or no fuss
in removing anything it has killed. For polecats I
prefer a 3in. or 4in. Dorset trap, carefully covered, and
according to the position of the bait it may be necessary
to employ a second one. If the victim of the vermin
against which the trap or traps be placed be a game-
bird, rabbit, or even hare, it is a good plan to so place
the traps that the stakes, chain, and springs lie beneath the bait when it is replaced and pegged down in
position. By putting the traps diagonally to the bait,
and with their springs parallel to one another, you
secure the best possible position for the jaws, and disturb no ground upon which the polecat is likely to
place its feet, except just where the jaws of the trap or
traps lie.

When trapping for polecats otherwise than as just
described, some bait or lure is necessary, as the chances
of taking them when running the hedgerows are somewhat remote. Something fresh-killed has far more
attraction for them than anything stale or putrid; so
that anything in the shape of small birds or rabbits,
fresh remains or liver—not entrails—of larger ones
serves the purpose excellently. Beyond this it is not
necessary to go in regard to baits, except to mention
that, as in the case of all the weasel tribe, the dead carcase of one of their kind possesses a remarkable attraction, as also that of the hedgehog.

When disposing baits of this kind, with the exception of the two last-named, it proves most successful if
they be suspended or fixed from 18in. to 2ft. above the
surface of the ground, the traps being placed beneath
where the vermin will place its feet when winding or

attempting to reach the bait. The most likely places should suggest themselves to the trapper, but certain spots alongside hedgerows, near gaps or gates, and against the trunks of large trees, prove most profitable. Polecats will frequent water-courses and more or less likely situations for traps offer themselves wherever there is a break in the ground, or where the water passes through hedgerow, fence, or paling.

The presence of polecats being established, run traps along the hedges, and such fencing as may divide covert from field or brake or woodland from woodland provides the most favourable opportunities for captures. Smaller traps—2½in. or 3in.—of the Dorset pattern, or some of the light steel traps figured previously, are the most suitable for the positions which offer, which, it is needless to say, will not be upon the ground surface, but upon the slopes of banks and such places which afford a mere foothold to the running vermin.

Ground Vermin : Stoats and Weasels.

The stoat and the weasel are assuredly too well known, both in regard to their appearance and usual habits, to require any lengthened reference in these respects. Still, they are often confounded one with the other, although differing in size, colouring, and, to some material extent, in habits, the misdeeds of the one being ascribed to the other, and immature stoats being classed as weasels, and vice versa. It will have to suffice for our purpose, however, to point out simply those points in their respective habits which directly affect the work of the trapper in seeking their capture.

Stoats are essentially gregarious in habit, and except during the breeding season, when the individual pairs take up separate existence, you may always expect to find other stoats in the neighbourhood of any whose haunts may be located. Not only will one or two pairs and their respective numerous offspring fraternise together, but frequently as many as twenty, thirty, or even forty will be found to harbour within the limits of as small an area as a quarter of an acre, or even less, of suitable covert. This will be some favoured spot in a wood, plantation, or brake, preferably where timber has been felled and stacked, and the undergrowth is again springing up; or it may be an extent of rough and broken ground in a field, along old and tumbledown stone walls overgrown with briar, bracken, and nettle, or along the broken and overgrown sides of a stream, the stoat being rather partial to water. Old gravel, stone, and lime pits also offer favoured shelter, as do any spots in which the features here named are combined or exemplified. The stoat rarely does more than accommodate the openings which exist naturally in such places to its wants, and is not given to working in the ground to the same extent as is the weasel, although it will not unfrequently adapt disused rabbit burrows or mole-runs to its particular requirements, and form additional surface openings to suit its own purposes.

The stoat is less of a night-hunter than the polecat, confining its marauding operations to the three or four hours before dark, and to the earlier ones of the morning. A good deal depends in this respect, however, upon the time of year, and warm and comparatively light nights usually witness stoats on the move. It is a quick and vigilant hunter, moves far afield, is a good and persistent climber, and, for its size, as ferocious and bloodthirsty a little rascal as ever cursed a game-covert. Any kind of game, ground or winged, comes kindly to its ken. It will also capture and partly devour field-mice, voles, shrews, small birds, and frogs, and is a bad enemy of woodcock nesting in our islands. Rats it will attack and kill, but not devour, and both young birds— especially game-chicks—and eggs also come within its list of provender.

Practically, the hunting ways of one species of weasel are those of the others, and the trapper should have no difficulty in picking up those of the stoat; in fact, I know no vermin so easy of observation once you hit off their retreat. Given, for instance, a stack of oak-bark or faggots in which stoats are known to harbour, if you take up a not too prominent position for observation within twenty or thirty yards, and maintain as absolute silence and stillness as is possible, the stoats will issue from their lairs and pass off in their several directions quite oblivious of your presence, thus providing every possible guide as to the proper whereabouts for placing the traps.

Stoats can be taken in either large Dorset or small run traps, and I am inclined to the opinion that, working upon the lines just referred to above, large Dorset traps of light construction, quick and tickle, will prove in even moderately adept hands as effective as anything else for general work. Stoats work a great deal along dry ditches, surface water-courses, when dry also, covert paths, and flushing trigs. They appear obliged to thread every gap and gate where an opening exists, and will persistently pass between gate and gate-post, leap up and over any ledge offering foothold, work amongst the stumps and stubs of felled trees, and mount to the first low fork of any growing ones. In all of these sites you can take stoats in the large traps when set in proper position with the merest covering over jaws and treadle, but with spring, etc., concealed. They will gallop along over a bed of dead leaves in the most unconcerned fashion, and thread their way through briar and dead brake in quite heedless manner. When trapping for them under these and most other circumstances, it is always most profitable to work the traps in series of twos and threes, because, hunting so closely in company, the distress of one stoat is sure to attract others. In the same way, if you take a bitch stoat what time the young are still with her, you are certain, by persistence, to secure most or all of the brood, for they are indefatigable searchers for a lost parent, notably the maternal one; whilst her mate, . though less persistent, is equally sure to endeavour to discover her whereabouts.

Success in taking stoats is mainly dependent upon close watching and observation of their movements, and wherever you find them running or working in other situations than those already named, the smaller traps, 2½in. or 3in. Dorset and the American-pattern ones, may be employed, but with baits. These may take the form of any of the items of stoat provender mentioned, or of such as were recommended for the polecat. The bait should always be suspended or pegged up six or nine inches above where the trap is concealed, or any

possible ledge upon which the vermin may be expected
to leap in order to secure the bait may also be utilised
with every advantage as the site for a trap. The bodies
of small birds fixed upon an overhanging bramble,
gorse, or other branch above a probable stoat's run are
a good lure, and the not too stale carcases of carrion
crows pegged down to the ground, with one or two traps
set adjacent, are a singular but successful bait for these
vermin.

The stoat is a very light-footed animal, and quick of
movement, and all traps must be set very tickle to take
them unfailingly; the springs must act quickly and
sharply, or you will miss your quarry time and again.
All traps for them should be set before noon, or they
will not be effective the same day; and when searching
for sites for them, pass a few yards parallel from the
run or path being followed, select your site, set the trap
or traps, return in your tracks, and continue to avoid,
as much as possible, the line the vermin may be expected to follow. When visiting the traps, the same
policy should be pursued.

From the trapper's point of view, there are few material differences in the habits of the weasel as compared
with the stoat, except that the former is less easy of
observation and usually more difficult to locate than the
latter. As a matter of fact, the habits and mode of life
of the weasel are distinctly different from those of the
stoat, but it is gregarious, issues forth on its daily
hunting expeditions in much the same manner, although, as a rule, the object of them differs. Considerably smaller than the stoat, it naturally follows that
the victims of its rapaciousness are correspondingly so,

and, although the mature pheasant and partridge occasionally fall to its ferocious nature, it is the young and notably the eggs upon which it mainly preys. Similarly to the stoat, it kills by blood-sucking, fixing itself on the jugular and throwing the hinder portion of its body on the back of its victim. It is thus easy to identify the work of either of these vermin. In the case of game-eggs, a single weasel will not be satisfied with one or two of a clutch—an ample meal—but will, as likely as not, break into all or nearly all of them, practically destroying the whole sitting, whilst it will, if possible, attack the sitting bird in the first instance.

Weasels frequent localities of similar character to those affected by stoats, but of more open and usually higher aspect, where plenty of sunshine reaches. Their partiality for stone walls, hedgerows, and the high banks alongside roads and paths is well known, so that, speaking generally, weasels may be sought for in less secluded and often quite frequented localities, compared with those where the stoat mostly congregates.

Weasels hunt much in company—sometimes as many as six or seven at a time—and they will then mob and kill leveret or rabbit with comparative ease. They are noisy over their work, and will screech and chatter when in close pursuit. Their marked antipathy to the mole, which they follow and search out in its own burrows, must not be overlooked, as many weasels may be taken from time to time when so hunting.

Upon the whole, the weasel is a far more difficult animal to trap successfully than the stoat. It is in every way less regular in its habits, and is as much a day hunter as any vermin going. Its activity commences with sunrise, and with occasional intervals for repose or feeding—it carries or drags much of its prey to its lair—continues until and often long after nightfall. I do not consider its scenting powers in any way equal to those of the stoat, and you may again and again see them, when hunting, raise themselves on their hindquarters to view possible quarry whose scent they have lost. Neither do they return so freely to prey they have killed and not carried off or consumed, so that in setting traps for them, it is necessary to weigh these facts and shape one's plans accordingly. It comes about for this reason that, as a rule, more weasels are taken in what I call permanent traps than in others. With these traps I shall have to deal at a later moment.

Once a large or small colony of weasels has been located, it is generally fairly easy to establish the range of their workings and trap for them accordingly. Dorset traps, 2in. to 2½in., working lightly and quickly, and small steel traps are the most serviceable ones to employ. For baits, small birds newly killed or any dead game chicks serve very well. They should have the skin lightly cut close round the shoulders, so that the neck covering can be drawn up towards the head, thus exposing the portion most attractive to the weasel. Peg or hang the bait 4in. above the treadle of the trap, and if any blood should fall upon the treadle, it will be of benefit rather than otherwise. Very careful and ticklish setting of the traps is necessary, and they must be covered as lightly and effectively as possible. The weasel chooses as clear and level a path as possible, following a rabbit run or anything which provides an unimpeded course. In this respect it differs materially from the stoat. It is, moreover, very prone to play about gaps and gateways, and suitable traps placed where there is a possibility of the weasels passing are usually productive. Made-up nests of stale or unfertile game eggs combined with the imitation article—i.e., one or two of the former to several of the latter—with one egg broken slightly to provide the necessary lure, may be placed in such sites as are considered likely to be visited by the vermin; and if ordinary hens' eggs be roughly broken up, contents and shell together, and a very slight trail be made of the result, leading to the made-up nest, it will successfully attract the vermin to the traps.

Wherever there exist any of those well-defined but usually narrow runs which lead from one rabbit's bolt-hole in the hedgerows to another, weasels working are almost sure to pass along them, and small run traps may be placed accordingly, not actually upon the run, but upon the edge of it, and a small bait laid pegged down a few inches on the inner side.

Much as weasels raid nests upon trees—they do not usually climb to those in bush, briar, or gorse—it is very difficult to take them when so engaged, unless the nest has only been partially despoiled: then a round trap set as lightly as the circumstances permit, with the remaining eggs poised upon the treadle, may prove effective. The trap must be of a small enough size to draw without touching the nest sides, and when setting fix the catch fairly stiffly and loosen it after the eggs are in position.

CHAPTER IX.

RATS.

It would be an unprofitable task to attempt to provide the intending trapper of rats, whether in field, homestead, or anywhere else, with a sufficiency of material hints as to their habits, because he would, probably, flatter himself that "everybody knows all about rats." I am candid enough to admit that, after many years' more or less constant warfare against these vermin I am still very far from knowing all about them. You can never gauge positively what will influence them in their movements and change of haunts. Certain general principles as to the movements, habits, and traits of these destructive rodents can be laid down, but, to get even with them in any way, they require watching and weighing up as to their intentions in every individual case, and without this the trapper will never succeed in making any appreciable reduction in their numbers. I will point out, as far as I can, what may influence them under certain circumstances, what they are likely to do under others, but no hard and fast line can be laid down, and every minutely local influence likely to affect their movements must be studied.

In connection with rats, too, I have come to the conclusion, after long and careful observation, that there are two varieties of the brown rat in these islands.* I cannot vouch for the limits of its distribution, but there is certainly a quite distinct, smaller, lighter, more rufous-coloured rat besides the ordinary brown rat, which at maturity assumes a rather grey than brown hue. I have discussed the subject with men quite competent to confirm or dispute the fact, and many have done the former and few the latter, pleading lack of observation as the reason. The mature rat of this variety never reaches the cumbersome, heavy form of the ordinary variety, is altogether more active, and has far more carnivorous than gramnivorous tastes. The variety is quite freely recognised in the Eastern Counties, where it receives the nickname of "higgler," from its predilection for young chicken and game. We used to come across them in the West of England, where they are generally distinguished as "hedge-rats," whilst a valued authority assures me that he knows the variety as existing in Cambridgeshire and its northerly adjoining counties. These higglers do not harbour in buildings, although they come into them for their prey and provender. They may be described correctly as field rats, and have their lairs in the hedgerows in summer and autumn, and in stack-bases, piles of faggots and brushwood, decayed timber, etc., in winter and spring. With this main exception they differ little in habits from the ordinary variety, except that, being more lithe and active, they move further afield.

The trapping of rats resolves itself into two separate

---

* It may be a variety of the black rat, which is much more common than supposed, and varies in colour to a bright brown at times.

descriptions of work—in the fields, woods, and preserves, and in and about the farm buildings and human
dwellings.   To be successful, very close, careful, and
skilled manipulation of the traps is required in the first
instance, and the avoidance of alarm and disturbance
of the rats unnecessarily in the second.   From the outset it must be made clear that, to achieve satisfactory
results, half-hearted measures will never avail.   It is
but rarely that you can anticipate the taking of a single
rat by employing only a single trap.   There are times
when it can be done, as, for instance, when a doe rat
with a hungry litter is pressed for food; but such cases
do not crop up regularly, and, as a rule, you must make
up your mind to the fact that the discovery of the workings of a single rat and what it has done is no assur-
ance that it will repeat the performance—rather the
reverse.   An instance will make my meaning more
clear, probably.   We will say that a rat has worked its
way into a game-coop and killed or taken one or two
chicks.   The ordinary idea is that it will come again;
traps are carefully put down for it for one or two nights
in succession, but the rat fails to return.   It, however,
plays the same game at another coop a night or two
after, but there were no traps there, precisely where
they should have been.   It amounts to this, that, as a
rule, to make sure of taking one rat, you must trap for
five or six.   If a rat raids one coop, prepare for its return at as many of the others as you can.   It entails
any amount of time and trouble, but it is the only way
to make sure.

Another main consideration in connection with the
trapping of rats is that the vermin work both singly and

in company. It is very difficult to determine when the latter is about to take place, but it is generally in connection with the formation of new workings. The fact that the doe rat when about to kindle hides her movements from the male or males, and withdraws to as remote a lair as is possible, usually identifies the nature of the single rat's working. She maintains wholly or partly her young until they are quite half-grown, and the litter, when foraging for itself, does so in company, and usually over the same ground. This provides one of the best opportunities, and if you can take the old one, it is quite easy to account for the whole of her litter one after another. By watching it is easy to determine the doe-rat with a litter. She will appear at dusk and keep on coming out and returning with what she may pick up in the way of provender. By carefully feeding her—maize in small and scattered quantities is the best draw—you can gradually lure her to your single trap. The youngsters easily follow on subsequent occasions.

Where rats work in company they are always living in company. It is not usually a very harmonious colony, and rows are frequent, which assist one in determining their whereabouts, and the evidence of their runs and holes provides the subsequent proof. It would entail far too much space to attempt to identify every possible site for rats' burrowings and workings. It is a question of seeking and finding. The best time for this is the dusk of the evening, whatever the time of year, for then the rats are well on the move, and can be watched to their lairs, which can in turn be duly investigated by daylight. I am, of course, treating of rats in the open at the moment. These outdoor, field, or woodland workings are always systematic, and usually more or less self-contained; not so those round homesteads and dwelling-places where rats burrow indiscriminately and apparently without purpose at times. Of these, more anon.

Now, in the meantime, as to traps. For general out-of-door field trapping there is nothing to beat the Dorset trap either in quite large size, 4in. or 4½in., or else in the small run form of 3in. or 2½in. size. For successful rat-trapping you must have the best, quickest, and cleanest working traps possible. They must set very low and very tickle, and be weather-proof in every respect.

When I say that the traps employed must be weather-proof in every respect, it must be remembered that traps set for rats in woodland, covert, field, etc., may have to remain in position for from two or three days to a week or more. During that time they are exposed to varying conditions of weather, and, unless the working parts are of such character as will ensure quick and clean action even after lengthened exposure, they might just as well remain unset at home. The flap or tongue must have a free lateral movement as well as the vertical one, and the same applies to the treadle where the catch works in the treadle standard. Rats are so wonderfully keen in winding the scent of human hands—they do not appear to notice that from the " cold boot "—that traps to be effective may have to remain a day or more before the scent wears off; consequently, it is quite impracticable to be continually resetting the traps with any chance of regular success.

In regard to the actual setting of the traps, there is nothing different in the mode of effecting this from the instructions I have already given, except that it is most necessary to disturb the ground as little as possible and to restore it to the same condition over the traps as it was before disturbance. The traps must be set with the greatest nicety, and to accomplish this I vary the process as follows:—Using a small, plain, thin bone paper-knife to support the treadle, I complete the setting of the trap without reference to the "tickleness" of such, leaving the flap and catch uncovered. Then, using the support in one hand, with a small, suitable piece of wood in the other, and carefully watching the catch, I adjust it to the degree of tickleness desired. The bone paper-knife slides easily from its position, and the catch and tongue are then finally covered. This plan saves an infinite amount of trouble, as the repeated springing of a lightly-set trap just when the finishing touches are being put to the operation is avoided.

Traps intended for rats may be kept well oiled in the working parts, but do not overdo this, otherwise they will clog. Unsalted hog's lard boiled up with neats-foot oil—one part to five—provides a good lubricant for the purpose. As it is necessary to deal with the trapping of rats in and around buildings, steadings, and the like separately, it will make for clearness and, I trust, success if I deal with rat-trapping in woodland and field under separate headings.

Trapping Rats in Woods and Covert.

The rats which affect the purlieus of our closer woodlands, for the most part game coverts, do not, as a rule,
take up their quarters within their limits unless they
are of large extent, and the neighbourhood of any
rides or dividing ditches or hedgerows, or even deeply
cut flushing trigs, provides them with suitable harbour.
Otherwise they lie on the outskirts in hedgerows, rough
ground, or by ditches and streams, and have their
runs or paths by which they enter the coverts in more
or less regular manner. When rats lie about ditches
or watercourses, wet or dry, they almost invariably
choose the lower situations and work upwards. In the
same way, when harbouring in the outer hedgerows
they pursue the same habit. It is consequently the
case that in connection with any woods, plantations, or
the like which occupy a sloping situation, most, if not
all, the effective work will be accomplished on the lower
sides. Similarly, in the case of more level ones, the
lairs of the rats will be found in or adjacent to any
depressions, dips, or faults in the ground.

Wherever pheasants exist and are fed in coverts, rats
will be attracted, the chief draw being the maize put
down and unconsumed by the game-birds; but beyond
this, the young of wild-nesting birds, their eggs, and
the other usual provender which contribute to furnish
the rats' larder also come into the category. As a most
general rule, there will be very little evidence forthcoming of rats' depredations under the circumstances,
except at nesting-time, when the frequent occurrence

of single eggs in unlikely places for the birds to have dropped them will point to the working of rats. What has to be done is to search out effectually their lairs and then trace the directions of their runs. This is not difficult of accomplishment, as the rats are sure to make for any soft or muddy places, and have their regular drinking places by the watercourses, where the peculiar markings of their feet are easily distinguishable.

The footmarks of the rat are so distinctive that they cannot be mistaken for those of any other small vermin. They resemble more the mark of an elongated hand when fully defined, but each foot has five small nodules upon it which always leave their imprint upon any surface sufficiently soft to receive it, even when that of the whole foot is not clearly defined. Advantage may be taken frequently of this fact to prove the movements of rats—an important item, because without this knowledge promiscuous trapping is very unproductive.

I have always found that, except in cases where actual depredations can be brought home to them, and the fact utilised for the purpose of taking them, the most satisfactory results follow when you feed the rats for a time or two before actually trapping for them. Grain, in the form of maize or wheat, is about the best means to employ for the purpose, but care must be taken that it is not taken by birds, and also not to use it too freely, as the rats frequently carry a good portion away, and then do not return. It may be suggested that a rat cannot carry much grain at a time, but as an instance I may mention that I have watched, personally, a rat from time to time during a period of nearly three hours, removing some maize, presumably grain by grain, from one spot to another some dozen yards distant.

Find out, in the first place, where the rats run : then place a little grain, thinly scattered, leading to a suitable trapping spot, where a half-handful may be closely spread.   If this be cleared off two nights in succession, put down your traps and bait each with a small heap placed over the loop of the spring where it encircles the jaws.   The traps should be 4in., and the vermin will be killed in the taking.   Draw the lure of thinly scattered grain to two or more traps after the second feeding, set the traps in the early morning, and if you take a rat in one the first night, reset and persevere for two or three nights in succession.   If nothing then results, try elsewhere.

Where rats have their workings and lair in hedgerows or banks, there is little good to be done by trapping at the actual burrows—for such they are—but you can frequently take them in small run traps at a little distance from the burrows either up or down the hedgerow, bank, or fault where they lie, or at a small distance out from the burrows in the direction regarded as most favourable.   In such cases a bait or lure should be employed, which may take the form of a dead chick or small bird hung upon a bush or fixed to a tree, or one or two broken eggs so placed as to be hidden from winged vermin passing overhead.   Upon the hedgerow or bank two traps suffice—one set close to the lure, the other a couple of yards from it in what is or might be the rat's run in that direction.   In the second instance named set three traps to each bait, one just under it, and two at angles a yard or so in the direction of the rat's lair. In each case the object of the additional traps is the same; if a capture be effected, other rats are sure to hurry towards the spot to see what the trouble is, and in all probability the one victim will bring others. The same plan may be pursued under other circumstances which will suggest themselves to the trapper.

As before mentioned, the doe rats go away to produce their young, hiding their nests from the males, and being most careful in concealing their whereabouts. When they kindle in woodlands, the nest will be, in all probability, at the base of an old and, possibly, hollow tree, in wood-stacks, or in stony or rocky places. It is not often that the lair can be detected until the young are old enough to partly fend for themselves, when they make their appearance for the first time or two. The doe and her progeny, however, soon leave the breeding quarters, and for the time being may seek different harbour almost every day until she casts them off. They are easily taken, comparatively speaking, at this period. As before mentioned, if the doe can be secured first, all the young can generally be accounted for by judicious feeding.

The fact that stoats and rats are always at enmity is frequently of service to the trapper in selecting the ground for his work, and the carcases of each prove good baits for the other. Then, again, neither stoats nor rats have any aversion to water, and the latter will frequently pass through the trickling water of a small ditch sooner than jump over it, as they easily can do. I have frequently taken rats in traps placed openly in

the shallow portions of such little water-courses where
the edges give evidence of the vermin coming to drink.
It must not be forgotten that rats are extremely thirsty
creatures, and in dry seasons the trapper should be able
to take ample advantage of the fact when working in
woodlands.

I hold the opinion that rats commit far less depreda-
tion in game coverts than is usually ascribed to them,
but they undoubtedly do a lot of damage at nesting-
time and during the period of early chickhood of pheasants. It is, however, the outlying nesting birds which
suffer most, for the chief reason that the woodland
nests are more closely looked after, and the rats are
more addicted to the hedgerows, spinneys, and odd bits
of plantation, etc., than to the main woods at such
time of year.

Trapping Rats in Field and Hedgerow.

A good deal depends upon the nature of the season
during the spring and early summer months to what
extent rats work the hedgerows. A wet period at that
season usually drives most of the vermin from the low-
lying lands, and it is then that they become numerous
and destructive in the spinneys and the hedgerows.
Except for breeding purposes, they do not fix upon permanent quarters for any length of time, but either lie
in any convenient corner or hole or, frequently, among
the dead debris at the bottom of hedge, brake, or any
low rough cover. You will frequently find them, too,
in rabbit burrows adjoining others still occu-
pied, and it is quite curious how at times rats and

rabbits will harbour alongside one another without interference by the former with the latter.

It is at this period and under these circumstances that rats work a deal of damage amongst game nests and game chicks. To a large extent the keepers should prevent this by searching out all such outlying nests and, in the case of pheasants, employing the eggs for hatching under hens. With partridges the case is different, but even in the case of the nests of these game-birds when placed in similar position, prevention is the best plan. As mentioned before, it is only when the depredations actually occur and evidence is obvious of the rats' work that the fact of their presence in field and hedgerow becomes plain. As a rule, once they start despoiling a nest, they will continue until the last egg is abstracted and carried away. Rats rarely break an egg until they get it to their lair, and a curious point to note is that the sitting bird will not always desert the nest at the first attack of a rat or rats, so that occasionally it is not possible to trap actually at the nest. In almost every instance rats fail to bring the eggs to their lair at the first attempt, and when you come across odd game-eggs in unlikely places, do not jump to the conclusion so frequently vouchsafed that the game-birds have dropped them promiscuously. In all probability a not very extended amount of time devoted to watching will prove rats as the delinquents, and if so one or more of the eggs may be utilised as baits.

Rats sometimes carry, but more often drag, eggs to their lairs; in the former case they tuck the egg up under the neck and support it by the upper portion of the fore-legs; in the latter they proceed half-backwards, half-sideways, drawing the egg with their fore-feet after them. It is little use expecting to secure the vermin when once on the move, as their course is erratic, and the traps should be set about the egg or eggs where they are found. Large traps are best, and usually three is the best number to use, placed in triangular fashion around the bait. The setting must be done very carefully, and the stake and chain of each trap be placed beneath it so that the jaws of one trap are at the extremity of the spring of the other.

It is not often that the sitting bird is herself attacked, but some wild pheasants will successfully beat off a single rat, and if the bird suffers, two or more of the vermin compass the attack and seize her by stealth. When the chicks suffer the attack is made at roosting-time, and the vermin kill and carry off as many of the youngsters as they can. The neck is bitten into and torn close to the breast-bone, and sometimes the brain is bitten into as well. Young pheasants are liable to be attacked and destroyed as long as they roost on the ground, and partridges practically till they reach a corresponding size.

If you can hit off instances of rats destroying game chicks before they remove all the victims to their lairs, as they do, they are fairly easily taken, using the dead chicks as bait. They must be left where found, and the traps set against them. In this case small traps will be found most convenient and effective.

Autumn sees a variation in the habits of rats round the hedgerows, as many come in and form regular workings in the banks, where they store up provender, and in which they pass the winter. They are fairly persistent in sticking to such winter quarters, and even ferreting will not cause them to quit them permanently. The provender stored will range from grain from the fields to potatoes and small mangolds, and the usual fruit of trees and hedges. It is from these burrows that they sally out and work into the farmer's outlying ricks, his potato and mangold clamps or caves, and other places of storage. At this period they are caught comparatively easily, when judiciously fed near the burrows, and I have found maize and small beetroot the most attractive and successful baits to employ, using the former with large traps to take and kill same time as previously described, and the latter as a bait likely to be carried off, and in connection with which smaller traps can be employed.

CHAPTER X.

RATS.—(Continued.)

The taking of rats in and about dwelling-houses, barns, stables, and the like, and the other odd buildings which go to make up the homestead or curtilage, is made easy at times by the employment of traps other than the Dorset pattern and its varieties, but very often the difficulties of employing the latter for lack of means to conceal them are not to be counter-balanced by the employment of traps of other principle. Unfortunately, many of these—most of them, in fact—only serve for a time (the rats learn to know and avoid them), but the Dorset trap is always effectual if properly used.

In connection with each and every sort of building which becomes infested with rats, it is frequently heard said that "they are running about all over the place." If carefully observed, it will be found that they are not; they are pursuing certain defined runs, and extend them if not checked. I place as much importance upon careful observance, before starting trapping, of the movements of the vermin as upon anything else, except careful and discriminate feeding of them before actually trapping. Of course, in granaries, stores, etc., where the rats' provender is spread out for them, so to speak, in inviting quantities in every direction, the matter is difficult, but where they have to seek their food assiduously, and it is scarce and not easily to be got at, the

matter is different. Under the former circumstances
and under others which will occur and suggest themselves, the wholesale employment of Dorset traps, covered or uncovered, serves the best purpose. The former
will require tying or fixing in an open and set position,
and leaving for from three days to a week before they are
placed in action. Tying up is a clumsy and troublesome matter. It is best for the purpose to provide one-
self with a number of what are termed U-pieces, which
will fit over the tongue and under the cross-piece of the
traps, and thus hold them as desired. Any good trap
manufacturer will furnish these to measurement at a
small cost, and of handier pattern than the local smith.

As traps of other patterns must be worked in connection with the Dorset ones for this class of rat-trapping,
I will describe the best and most effective of these before
going further into the actual application of them to the
work in hand.

One of the most useful and effective traps for rats,
and in many ways for other small vermin is Everitt's
Patent, of which I give illustrations in Figs. 23 and 24.
The principle of the trap is made sufficiently clear to
render superfluous any detailed account of its mode of
working. It is in regard to the employment and application of it that some remarks may prove useful. The
trap is sprung by the vermin attempting to pass through
it, when they place their feet on and depress the treadle.
It can be worked with or without a bait; in the former
case the bait is attached to or suspended upon the inside
of the small metal tunnel, or it may be placed upon the
ground simply to draw the vermin through and thus
cause their undoing. When employing these traps for

rats whose runs enter buildings, or where they have worked into pens, etc., the traps should be placed against the best worked holes and others may be blocked up. The jaws and treadle should be covered thoroughly, but lightly, with coarse sawdust or chaff, and the same material extended some little distance on each side of the trap. Thus, if one be placed against a hole through a granary partition or thin parting-wall, the material used for concealing the trap should be scattered upon the ground leading to the rat-hole upon the outside as well as the inside, otherwise the vermin

Fig. 23.

EVERITT'S PATENT TRAP (SET).

become chary of entering, and seek other runs. It is often of assistance if the trap be covered with a piece of old sacking, hay, straw, or other material, whilst when employed out of doors, any suitable covering which the surroundings may suggest adds to the efficiency of the traps.

Their employment in the numberless situations of the kind named is always pregnant with good results, but sometimes, where places are honeycombed by rat runs, it is impossible to cover all with traps or stop up those not provided with them effectually. In such cases opportunity must be made where it does not exist, and to this end some lengths of drain-pipe, wooden guttering, or similar means for providing small tunnels must be arranged for the vermin to run through. This they are very prone to do, and if fed carefully will soon make a frequent practice of it. The idea in its simplest form is to place two lengths of drain-pipe about 4in. diameter end on to one another, but leaving a gap between them of sufficient width to admit an Everitt's trap. Scatter some of the covering material to be used within the pipes and across the gap, adding a little maize or other

Fig. 24.

EVERITT'S PATENT TRAP (SPRUNG).

corn to it. As soon as the vermin feed freely, set the trap in the gap, and repeat it after each capture. Any amount of variations of this idea occur, and will suggest themselves to the astute trapper, as well as many other sites where they can be placed with immunity to other animals than vermin.

In connection with these traps I have employed locust beans—good new season ones, not old, stale, maggot-eaten husks such as are often supplied—as a bait for rats, tying the beans in the roof of the trap. It may be remarked incidentally with advantage that locust beans are capital bait for rats in buildings, and the fresh meal made from these beans, mixed with chaff, or even sawdust, is an excellent lure for the vermin.

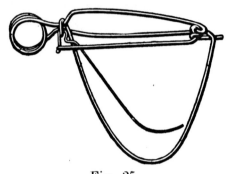

Fig. 25.

STOP-THIEF TRAP.

Both the beans and meal sufficiently new are difficult to obtain locally, but they are always to be had from or

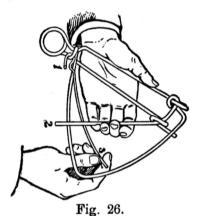

Fig. 26.

STOP-THIEF TRAP.
How to set it.

through corn-chandlers in the leading ports. Old beans or stale meal are of little or no use.

Another very useful trap for rats in and about buildings, and occasionally along the hedgerows, ricks, etc., is the "Stop Thief" trap, which is also shown in Figs. 25 and 26. This trap is of steel wire, and the action may be understood on reference to the cuts. The small wire in the lower portion of the loop is the trigger; this, on being pressed by the feet of the vermin passing through, releases the striker (the thicker horizontal wire above), which, acted upon by the coiled spring, flies violently down, killing the victim instantly. These

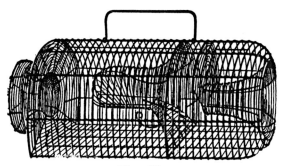

Fig. 27.

traps can be placed almost anywhere where rats pass through an aperture of whatever kind. No bait is required, and, as a rule, nothing is gained by employing one except to lure the rats to certain holes and runs where the traps may be placed in preference to others.

There are a couple of traps, a box, and a tunnel trap made by Messrs. Wm. Burgess and Co., of Malvern Wells, which may be used for rats with advantage, as well as for other vermin, but which I shall figure and describe at a later date, when dealing with "permanent" traps. This firm supplies an exceedingly effective wire cage trap for rats (Fig. 27) at a very reason-

able price. It is one of the best cage traps there is.
Its construction is made plain in the illustration, and
when baited at both ends, as it can be, and after having
been left open so as to feed the rats for a night or two,
it may be trusted to take as many rats as there is room
for in it.

Another very good litile trap, the "Out o' Sight"
trap, as it is called, is shown at Fig. 28. It is useful
for placing upon walls, rafters, and other elevated
places where rats run and where other traps cannot be

Fig. 28.
" OUT O' SIGHT " TRAP.

disposed with advantage. It works without a bait, by
the mere fact of the vermin running over it.

Another good trap is the " Pennsylvania " rat trap
(see Fig. 29), which may be placed in all kinds of odd
corners, and is not affected by damp or wet weather.
It can remain set for months, if necessary, and still
remain thoroughly effective and quick in its action.

Besides the traps which have been figured and described as peculiarly adapted for taking rats in and
around buildings, etc., there are several designs of
cage traps, constructed of wire, specially suited to
these vermin. Several more or less effective designs
are obtainable, but for the most part they possess the

defect that not more than one capture can be secured at
one setting of the trap. When it comes to putting
down a dozen or more at a time, the expense is large,
and the process troublesome. One form of cage rat-
trap I have employed with conspicuous success at times
may be referred to more particularly. It consists of a

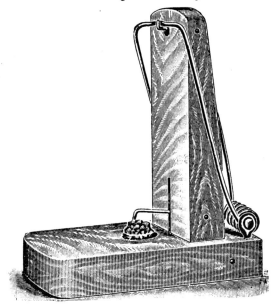

Fig. 29.

PENNSYLVANIA RAT TRAP.

wire cage about 2ft. 6in. square by 5in. high. In the
centre is a small compartment, about 8in. square, open
at the top, into which a second small cage can be fitted.
This latter holds one or more live rats as decoy. At
each corner of the outer cage is a small tunnel entrance
with a flap to close it after a rat has pushed its way in.
There is no spring or other contrivance, and by employ-

H

ing a little grain as a lure to and through
these entries, the vermin enter freely to join the decoys,
which are, of course, visible to them.   These traps can
be put down and left for several days, provided food
and water are supplied to the decoy rat or rats.   This
can be done, as I did it, by fixing small tin receptacles,
such as are fitted to bird-cages, within the decoy cage.
The same should be done in the trap proper, if it be
not intended to visit it and take out any caught rats
at least every second day, as it is both needlessly cruel and detracts from the effectiveness of the
trap if rats be allowed to die within it.   These wire
traps are obtainable from most ironmongers who deal in
sporting sundries, but I am unaware of the names of
the manufacturers who produce them.

I do not consider that any useful purpose would be
served by alluding to and giving descriptions of any
others of the very numerous array of traps designed for
the taking of rats.   Not many of them are really useful,
and most of them are less effective than those to which
I have already referred.   There are, moreover, many
ways of taking these vermin under special circumstances in contrivances more or less ingenious.   The
employment of the principle of the pitfall in this respect
may be alluded to, however, as being very useful at
times.   A barrel with a swinging cover working very
lightly on two pivots, and containing a few inches of
water, sufficient to drown any victims falling into it, is
the best manner of applying it, and may be employed
in many positions, both indoors and outdoors, in places
where rats are numerous and run freely.

CHAPTER XI.

WILD CATS.

The true wild cat exists still in Wales, the North of England, and in most of those parts of Scotland where the nature of the country is such as to forbid the intrusion of the agriculturist. It is an open question whether all the wild cats reported as being killed in Scotland are really specimens of the true species Felis sylvestris. Anyhow, they are certainly wild enough and as destructive as cats, wild or otherwise, notoriously are within the limits of the game preserve. It is a fact generally accepted by zoologists that our domestic cats are descended, or have ascended, from the Egyptian species, and none directly or indirectly from the indigenous one. Many of the photographs of wild cats caught in Scotland so closely portray the wild cat of Egypt that one is tempted to believe that there may be two species of wild cat now in Scotland—the representatives of the original stock and a race of others of the Egyptian type reverted to by the offspring of domestic tabbies gone woefully astray. Inasmuch as the true wild cat does not interbreed with the domestic variety gone wild, there can be no suggestion of a cross between them

It is scarcely necessary to provide any detailed account of the haunts and habits of the wild cat, because the country over which it is still existent is of so pro-

nounced a character that when one states that it com-
prises some of the wildest and most remote portions of
the less frequented parts of Scotland, northern England, and Wales, and, I believe, occasionally Ireland,
the general character of its haunts is easily established.
Its home is amongst the fern, bracken, and heather-
grown rocks, often in difficultly accessible places and
amidst the shadows of the thicker and remoter woodlands.   For the most part a night-hunter, the wild cat
is rarely seen in full day-time, but at early morn and in
the dusk of the evening the keeper or the trapper in the
districts named may come across it chance-wise.   As a
rule, however, it is mainly by its misdeeds that the wild
cat makes its presence known and provides the signs by
which may be traced the whereabouts of its lair, which,
except at the time when it is rearing its young, is very
difficult of precise location.   It is for the most part only
at such times that the wild cat carries its prey to its
lair; at others it takes its meal where it effects the capture of its victim, and it is in the debris of fur and
feather which it leaves behind it that we have the evidence of its being in the neighbourhood.   The wild cat,
in common with most other vermin, kills far more than
it can consume, and may or may not return to the half-
eaten carcases of any birds, hares, or rabbits it may
have destroyed.   Its hunting efforts must have had poor
or no results subsequently if it seeks out and returns to
the remains of a previous meal.   It is consequently not
usually assumed that traps set against such when discovered will prove effective, although they may do so.
The wild cat hunts very far afield from its lair and does
not make a practice of passing over the same ground or

working in the same direction, but if winding a previous kill of its own may draw upon it, but not actually go to it.

The Highland keeper—and there is probably no more adept class nor better trappers in the kingdom—in dealing with the wild cat reasons as to its movements rather by analogy than direct inference, and places his traps in positions where cats are likely to be rather than where they have been. You want a good deal of local knowledge in order to work upon these lines, and it is only by constant coming and going to and fro, and the exercise of close habits of observation whilst so doing, that the necessary insight into the matter can be obtained.

The usual trap employed for taking the wild cat is a large Dorset one, which, viewing the fact that the animal when taken is valuable dead or alive, are usually very strongly holding, not too closely jawed, quickly-striking traps. They must be really weather-proof—I have previously explained the term as applied to traps—and may have to remain set (and tickle at that) for days on end in the same places. No more shy, wary, and cunning creature exists among vermin than the wild cat, and the trapper has much to overcome in these respects.

It is a curious fact that almost equal numbers of them—they do not amount to very many in the year over the whole country—are taken by chance and by traps placed specially for them. It is in trapping for other vermin, and notably for rabbits, that the former happenings arise, and beyond stating the fact there is nothing more to be said in the direction named. In the latter instance, however, detailed information is necessary   If you have ever taken notice how a domestic cat fiddles with a piece of food thrown to it before it settles down to take hold and gnaw it, you have a good example of how a wild cat treats any bait put down for it.   It will wind it, work round at a distance, draw upon it from several points, possibly never approaching within a yard or two, and as likely as not leave it for the time being to return and repeat the performance, or maybe not return at all if its suspicions be aroused.   If, on the other hand, the bait be taken, it will be from behind probably, and be seized by the shoulders or neck, be it fur or feather.   It follows, therefore, when setting for a wild cat, that the trap placed at the back of the bait is chiefly to be relied upon, but other traps should be placed at what may be termed the "avenues of approach" a yard or more from the bait, and not close enough to one another for the cat to become caught in more than one of them.   For bait any fresh-killed bird, wild pigeon, wildfowl, or game-bird is the best amongst feather, and a rabbit or leveret otherwise.   It is best to peg it down, unless placed where it would not be seen by winged vermin passing over.   To enumerate all the possible likely places where traps may be set would be impracticable.   They must suggest themselves, but it may be mentioned that wild cats greatly affect the sides of water-courses, the gullies, the broken ground, and any tangled piece of bracken and briar and heather. Naturally, wherever the game frequents, wild cats will forage, but they are hot in pursuit of line quarry, and lose most of their wariness and caution when close upon it.   The body of a dead fox or dead cat, wild or tame, is an effective lure for them, and may always be utilised for the purpose when available.

It must be remembered that, as a rule, the home of the wild cat is far from the haunts of men, and being so far afield, the tendency is to neglect traps put down for them. It should be possible—or made so, anyhow—to visit them every second, or needs be every third day.

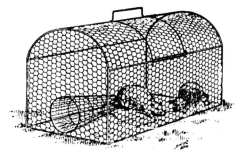

A USEFUL FUNNEL CAGE-TRAP.

As a rule, however, if a field glass be employed, it is easy to know if a capture be made, as by the presence of birds making a considerable commotion round the spot, mocking their arch-enemy in distress, no doubt.

It is practically impossible to take a mature wild cat in a box or cage trap, but the kittens will enter them if the mother be taken when they are of tender age and just foraging for themselves.

CHAPTER XII.

POACHING DOGS AND CATS.

The domestic feline which takes to a wild or semi-wild life and rears a litter of kittens in a rabbit burrow to plague and infest the preserve, or the almost equally destructive ordinary domestic cat which goes poaching on its own accord or by encouragement of its owner, are equally to be destroyed whenever chance offers.

These brutes make such a horrible row when taken in traps of the ordinary Dorset type, alarming everybody and everything within furlongs of their whereabouts, that it is far better to employ either the "Hugger" type of trap, such as I have already figured and described, or one or other form of box-trap, of which I shall give full particulars at a subsequent date. The domestic cat which takes to a wholly wild life out of doors soon becomes very wary, shy, and fearsome, and difficult to capture. The ordinary poaching cat is, however, different, and falls an early victim. Wherever rabbits are trapped, each or other of these vermin—for such poaching cats are—is sure to get into the traps placed for the conies. They appear to be attracted always at such times, and can generally be accounted for by the trapper. They accomplish any amount of injury to rabbits already caught, killing and mauling them in the traps so as to render them hopelessly useless except as baits or lures for themselves.

Poaching cats are very destructive to young game, furred and feathered, and also to the sitting game-birds. They are, however, easily lured to any baited trap, and, being in the habit of pursuing almost the same line when setting out on their marauding expeditions, a little, even casual, observation will show where they may be trapped for. Almost any available bait will suffice for both " Hugger " and box-traps, but although fish is frequently recommended, you will find that they will ignore it except in close proximity to the dwelling-house or homestead. The use of valerian may be recommended for poaching cats, and both box and " Hugger " traps may be " dressed " with it as attraction. It must be applied, however, within the former, and not on the outside.

No precise instructions should be necessary as to where to place traps for poaching cats. The disposal of box-traps for them is not fraught with any particular difficulty, but the " Hugger " traps are somewhat dangerous articles where dogs are concerned, and a warning in this direction is advisable. The habit which cats possess of creeping and drawing themselves through any small runs amongst briars and other low covert may be taken advantage of, but the traps should always be placed so that the bait is easily accessible and can be taken with the mouth and not have to be drawn out by the vermin's paws.

It is necessary to discriminate between those dogs which poach regularly and others which only do so occasionally, because the indiscriminate taking of dogs in traps is not altogether judicious, and may land one into serious trouble. There are, however, up and down the country hundreds of what may be called professional poaching dogs which exist solely upon what they can pick up in the preserves and elsewhere. The man who is engaged in trapping rabbits and vermin is sure to meet with them and suffer indirectly from their depredations. These brutes are for the most part of a mongrel sheepdog type, owned, if owned at all, by those who have no possible use for them, except as a reason for the employment of bad language and the administering of stray kicks. They are usually sleepy and listless by day, but develop symptoms of activity and intelligence towards night-time. As a rule it is difficult to identify the owners of regular poaching dogs, as the brutes work far afield from their homes. This is an advantage to anyone trapping them, as he is not likely to be bothered by inquiries.

The true poaching dog is a most unmitigated nuisance, and fearfully destructive. It must be added that dogs which run riot occasionally are equally so at times, and if they get into trouble in the form of traps placed for others. the blame does not lie with the man who put them down.

The manner of dealing with the regular poaching dog depends upon circumstances. Larger specimens of the tribe do not make much fuss when taken in ordinary traps, but the smaller ones sometimes make a tremendous hubbub. Speaking generally, the regular poaching dog begins again where it left off, and if you find evidence of their work, and possibly spot them at or near the place, it is fairly certain that they will, if not seriously interfered with, come back to the same spot. Their chief depredations will be the taking of rabbits from traps or snares, failing which they will mouth and maul and partly consume them, abjuring the head, as a rule—just the opposite to the methods of the poaching cat. Then they will frequent the keeper's rearing-fields, get amongst his young birds when first turned away in the coverts, and also at an earlier season champ up any nest of eggs or young birds they may come across, and chop up young rabbits and leverets.

Luckily, a poaching dog will come to almost any lure or bait placed in any situation, so that you can lay out to take them in precisely the spot most suitable for the purpose. Best of all baits are liver and the entrails of poultry. The liver should not be allowed to dry off, for then it emits very little odour. It requires to be kept in a warm, damp place until flabbily putrid; once in this desirable condition, it will retain its value for the purpose for some days. In the same way the fowl bait must be treated. Either of these will attract a passing poaching dog from any quest it may be on. The trap to be used—one well staked down, using two stakes and chains if considered necessary—is a large Dorset trap; 5in. or 6in. jaws is not too much width, but they should not rise very high. If employing two chains, do not extend them in the same line as the trap, but place each and its attached stake at right angles to that line; but the latter must have a swivel attached to it between the chain ends and the S-hook. In this manner there is no play for the dog to jump upwards, as it does when caught, and it is held fast without the chance of breaking bone—rather an important matter if one of any value be taken.

The best places, from more than one point of view,

for traps for poaching dogs are in any ditches, depressions, or breaks in the ground below the level of its surface. Whether provided with low covert or not is immaterial, as you can always draw a dog down into such spots far more easily than up on to a bank or rising ground : the scent is stronger and more diffused, and the attraction greater. Naturally, any baited traps put down must not be sufficiently near a highway to lure a dog from it, and in choosing sites for the traps, select those most free from observation.

Of course, traps of the "Hugger" type may be employed if you are sure of your dog and are content that, whatever the marauder, it shall cease to live for its pains. But I am not in love with these traps, for this particular reason, and prefer the Dorset type, as you can then settle your captive or release it, as the case may warrant. There are, however, occasions when the "Hugger" traps may be employed with every confidence that they will only take and kill the animal intended.

Poaching dogs are difficult to get into box-traps, but they will enter the double-ended ones at times if of sufficient size and properly placed in a gap otherwise filled up, for instance, or in dry gutters running through a hedgerow ard such-like not improbable places for anything of the kind to occur. The correct type I will figure and describe on a subsequent occasion.

CHAPTER XIII.

TRAPPING FOXES

The taking of foxes in traps may not be recognised as a legitimate proceeding over a very wide area of these islands, but wherever hunting the fox with hounds does not obtain and it is sought to preserve game it is necessary at times to limit the depredations of foxes by hunting them out with terriers, digging, or, as a final resource, by trapping. There exist still most extensive districts in various parts of the country where fox-hunting is quite out of the question, and in such districts the trapper is called upon regularly to exercise his craft in limiting the number of foxes. I am not one of those prejudiced folks who, because they rear a few hundred pheasants, would destroy every fox in the county, and, regarding "the varmint" as a beast of chase, I have always made it a point to take any foxes with as little injury as possible and transfer them, by sale or gift, to some hunting country where they would be welcome I think this arrangement should be carried out wherever feasible. With the making of these few preliminary remarks to clear the ground we can now get to work

Wherever foxes are trapped for regularly two sets of conditions influence the mode of operations. In the first place traps are put down without reference to any particular delinquencies upon the part of the vermin, but with a view to taking any which may be upon the move; in the second place, some particular depredations amongst game, or maybe poultry, call for special attention, and so special means must be adopted for dealing with the offender. Some general idea of how to go to work in each instance should serve to guide the trapper in the right direction without going into details of every possible set of circumstances under which foxes may be trapped.

The best possible trap for the purpose is a best quality 4in. Dorset trap fitted with strong chain, two swivels, and an extra strong and long stake varying from 18in. to 2ft., according to the nature of the soil. It is advisable also to drive in the stake at a slight angle. The traps must hold strongly and strike hard, as foxes are almost invariably taken across the pad in traps of the size named. As a rule any injury done is merely superficial and easily submits to treatment. Of some scores taken in this way I cannot remember having had to destroy more than one or two on account of injury thus caused. If you employ larger traps they are likely to break bone or inflict serious injury. They must lie very low and the springs, if of the flat description, correspondingly so. The wire-spring traps are, however. much the best to employ, because it is unnecessary to disturb the ground to so great an extent as with the others. The actual setting requires no particular description, the points to be observed being that a fox's tread is very light—often a mere touch—and that unless the trap is perfectly concealed and practically no visible sign left of the ground having been disturbed, there is little or no chance of effecting a capture. It is necessary, as a rule, to anticipate that traps placed for foxes may have to remain set for some days--- a week or more; consequently, when putting them down the nature of the surface of the ground must be considered because upon that depends how long the covering placed over them can stand without exposing their presence to the vermin.

The fox and its ways, its haunts, and habits are so hedged around with the imaginative outpourings of the purveyors of so-called popular natural history that if the tyro in trapping believed one-tenth of all that has been written, he might give up any attempts to take it in traps which necessity might advise or suggest. If we take Reynard as he—or she—is in plain and sober fact, he is a most difficult animal to trap, and the skilled trapper, brimful of woodcraft and similar knowledge, often finds himself at fault—as well he might. On the other hand, if you be content to sink all you think you have learnt upon the subject and trust to your own powers of observation and the piecing together of Nature's puzzle, it will be found that there is as much routine and as much following of a seemingly blind instinct in the fox as there is in any other creature against which the hand of man is everlastingly raised.

Once you get amongst where foxes run and secure a fair working idea of their ways and the places they habit, you will not have much difficulty in taking them. They have their runs, their beats, their regular ways, and it will appear strange that an animal so cunning apparently and possessed of so much intelligence should ever be taken. There is, however, a peculiar persistency about these and other predatory creatures of pursuing the same path. Of course, they break away from it, but to return; and it is this trait in their habits which enables the trapper to secure them. A fox's run, whether in covert, field, across moorland, brae or fell, is always fairly well marked to those who know, and it is in the proximity of the runs that traps may be set with most probable success. Of the signs which point out these runs it is difficult to write without occupying undue space. However, you will discover here and there more or less regular dropping-places; you will find where the fox or foxes have couched temporarily, but more or less repeatedly; your olfactory nerves will tell of other visits; and, finally, there will be evidence in the form of fleck and feather, and possibly more solid remains of their victims.

It is in the neighbourhood of or alongside these runs that trapping operations must be carried on. It is really of small use trying to effect captures elsewhere when working on general lines, because unless the regular haunts of the foxes can be located, the occasional ones offer no opportunities for working traps. Obviously a great deal depends upon the district in regard to the nature of a fox run. As a rule it is selected with a view to the security of the varmint whilst on the move, and the more frequented the ground over which they work the more regular are their movements. Given, however, districts which are but little frequented except by keepers on somewhat occasional rounds and at shooting time, and it will be found that the foxes exercise little discrimination in choosing the paths they pursue. There are places which, if you watch them regularly, you will find continually patronised by foxes just as they pass over very well marked paths. Whilst at or covering either they are, however, at their wariest, and it is most difficult to take the vermin immediately upon them. It is only when they have assured themselves, as one may put it, that there is no immediate danger at hand that they pass into pursuit and throw off some of their fearsomeness. It is then upon the ground which leads off from the runs in many directions that general trapping may be undertaken. You will also discover for yourself that the unhunted fox—or, rather, the fox in unhunted districts—possesses points of observation to which it resorts from time to time, and from which a view over a considerable area is obtainable. The fox draws as much information as to possible danger from the movements and cries of birds near and at a distance as from anything else, and frequently shapes its course accordingly.

Having ascertained in a general way the probable movement of the foxes, you can then start out with a view to trapping them. It is impossible within reasonable limits to specify in detail the features of every typical spot suitable for the position of one or more traps. I will, however, cite one or two as a guide to the selection of others. We will take first the instance of a rough covert, an outlying one probably, occupying a large expanse of broken ground. Through this runs a watercourse, following the trend of the ground, and "made up" on its lower side. It causes an opening in what covert there is a couple or more yards wide. Along here the foxes are accustomed to run. Pass along it till there is a break in the covert on one side or the other showing a fairly open piece of ground, where the brake

I

or undergrowth is sparse and reaching maybe a dozen or fifteen yards into the thicker growth. At the extremity or on one or either side there will be a small level space a square yard or so in extent and well backed by thick growth. This should prove as likely a site for a well-placed trap as can be desired. For bait choose the likeliest item that might occur in such a place--a woodpigeon, a rabbit, or something of the kind. Treat the bait as if it had been killed and torn by a hawk, scattering feather or fleck around after you have set your trap, but pegging the bait down securely. Expose the torn flesh and a little of the entrail, and set your trap about a foot out from the bait, which should lie again about a foot from the covert at its back. Set a second trap in the space between. The traps will probably be placed in a surrounding of somewhat dry, possibly mossy, verdure, which is in favour of the trapper, as they may have to lie a day or two. The traps should be put down early in the day after the dew is off, and it may be that a capture results the same evening or during the night, perhaps not for a day or two.

Along the stretch of watercourse will be other such sites, and they may be provided accordingly, but do not overdo it, and vary the bait and idea of setting. A dead and decaying hedgehog will lure the fox from its path, but it will no more than draw upon and wind it, so the traps placed must be in the probable path of the fox towards the lure. The body of a dead cat, stale or putrid, is a tremendous attraction, and suitable for use at such a spot as described. Simply draw the defunct grimalkin by a cord (easily detached) to the site chosen and leave it there for a couple of days. You will soon know on visiting it if the foxes have found it out, and then place two, or even three, traps round about it, but at least six feet from one another. If you effect a capture try again, or convey the remains to another site and repeat the process.

There are often breaks in fir plantations where, for some reason or other—usually a rise of water to the surface, but not enough to be classed as a spring— the trees have not grown. Generally a thick, velvety green sward covers the opening, a favourite play-place for rabbits, sunning-place for feathered game, and a squatting pitch for the foxes. A dead rabbit deftly set up in crouching form and position, with a trap on each side towards the tail end of the bait, is a good lure in such a place.

Upon the open moorland where there is a break in the ground, a small bluff, in fact, the upper surface begrown with strong heather, the lower running away in a bank of rotten granite sand, is another fruitful site for traps—one upon an open heather-free portion of the upper surface and another at the foot of a sand-run beneath. Almost any bird torn and the feathers scattered about will serve as bait. Peg it in position between the trap above and the one below.

These are all typical spots for foxes when traps are being used generally against them, but there are a score and more similar which the intelligent exercise of his knowledge will prompt the trapper to utilise for his purpose.

Hitherto the trapping of foxes in a general way upon lands where they cannot be considered other than vermin has received attention. We must now come to the subject of taking them upon such preserves as, although in no wise coming within the limits of hunting countries, provide for a certain amount of protection being extended to the foxes so long as they do not interfere seriously with the game. There are, no doubt, multitudinous instances where depredations by other vermin, poaching dogs and cats, are placed to the discredit of the foxes. Upon the other hand, they are most destructive at times, most persistent in their evil-doing, and most difficult to deal with. There are three certain periods in the foxes' year when the spirit of destruction is strongest upon them—at clicketing time, when the vixens are cubbing and have cubs, and during periods of the year when food runs scarce, namely, the winter months and early spring. Candidly speaking, it is most difficult to maintain foxes and game without catching the former when they become active. It is, however, as I have stated, quite feasible to trap them without doing serious injury.

When you come to trapping individual foxes which have committed certain depredations, the chief difficulty arises from the fact that a fox, except under certain occasional conditions, rarely returns immediately to the scene of them. If it abandon a portion of its prey, it is unlikely to return to it, although it may return to the neighbourhood of its exploits. Thus it is that any such abandoned prey serves little purpose as a lure or bait. At rabbit-trapping time foxes may continually go over your traps, taking a rabbit here and hopelessly damaging one there; but they do not come again to the same places. In the same way with winged game. You will find evidence of their work, but they do not within practicable time revisit the scene of their exploits. These remarks are necessary to make it clear how and when to set to work to trap the doer of the damage. In connection with rabbits it will be found generally that these themselves furnish a good guide to the movements of the fox, and you must work for it accordingly. I have found that one of the best baits and lures for foxes which molest the rabbits in warrens and such warren-like portions of rough preserves where the conies are in greatest evidence is a newly-killed one used as follows: Place the rabbit by its forelegs in a trap, and stake the trap down on a hedgerow, so that the trap and rabbit in it hang down the side, the rabbit's head and shoulders being about two feet from the level of the ground beneath. It does not matter that the other portion is nearer the ground. The fox will reach up for the shoulders and head of the lure. About six to nine inches outward from where the rabbit hangs down, and upon the level of the ground, place your trap where the varmint is likely to set its pads. I have worked the same manœuvre successfully under varying conditions wherever I have been pestered by foxes interfering with rabbit-trapping operations. It is necessary to repeat, however, that anything of the kind must be done not exactly where the varmint has committed depredations, but in similar places, where it will most probably come subsequently.

The same idea must prompt your workings in connection with damage done to winged game—pheasants, partridges, grouse, or duck. I stopped more than one fox one autumn-time with the body of an old blackcock used in this manner, but it was secured by the legs in

the trap and hung from a high bank, so that the head
was the necessary height from the ground, and the body
unattainable from the top of the hedgerow.   The body
of a woodpigeon disposed a few feet from the
ground in the lower branches, but close to the trunk, of
a fir-tree—larch, spruce, or pine—with one or two
traps set on opposite sides of, and about nine inches
out from, the tree-stem, is also effective.   Tear a small
bunch of feathers from the back, and poise the bait

Fig. 30.

HUMANE TRAP, WITH SPIRAL-SPRING CHAIN.

breast upwards, scattering the feathers where they
might be expected to lie if the bird had fallen into the
position in which it is placed.

At this point I give an illustration, Fig. 30, of a very
useful form of trap made by A. A. Cruickshank, of Glas-
gow, with a view of preventing broken bones in the animal caught in it, and which may with advantage be employed for taking foxes under the conditions now being
discussed.   The jaws of the trap are furnished with flat
rubber let into them, whilst the chain has a strong,

moderately stiff spiral spring provided. The jaws hold very fast, and the spiral counteracts the ill-effects produced by the fox's habit of jumping upwards and outwards when caught. Traps with at least 4½in. or 5in. jaws are necessary, so that the varmint may be taken and held above the pad. The spiral spring has the further effect of restraining considerably the movement of the fox when caught. It is generally found that, when taken in traps thus provided, the fox restrains itself far more than is usually the case.

It is next to impossible to make any haul of foxes when on the run at clicketing time. Unless the vixen go blundering into traps put down for other things, she is rarely taken, and yet the damage they do at such times is frequently almost inconceivable, notably amongst poultry. For pure wantonness in killing there is nothing to compete with them at such times, when the opportunity offers; but as the first visit is usually the last as well, there is little chance of laying specially for them.

CHAPTER XIV.

TRAPPING HAWKS.

The continual and, to a large extent, useless and wanton warfare which has been waged against the hawk tribe by ignorant people, mainly of the gamekeeper class, has resulted not only in an enormous reduction in the numbers of these predatory birds, but has almost completed the extinction of several varieties. Even now a certain class of keeper cannot be brought to believe that, because a bird is of the hawk tribe, it is not necessarily injurious and in need of immediate killing. In the same way, they will swear upon seventeen Bibles that the cuckoo destroys eggs and young game, because it resembles in some respects the sparrow-hawk and quarters its ground in the same manner, although the prey in view is vastly different.

Speaking generally, the number of hawks really inimical to the interests of the game-preserver—and, it may be added, the poultry-keeper in some districts— which are more or less plentiful over the more closely cultivated portion of the kingdom may be counted on the fingers of one hand. If we include the wilder districts and less cultivated areas, we are bound to include some of the larger ones. It is a moot question whether the comparatively few predatory hawks which affect our grouse moors are really inimical to the grouse preserver's interests. Personally, I would extend the

greatest possible leniency to the hawks and falcons of
these islands, but there are occasions continually arriv-
ing when the damage they do to game is very serious,
and there remains no other remedy than to destroy
them : and for this purpose traps are the most effective
means.

The sparrow-hawk and the hen-harrier regularly, the
marsh-harrier and the kestrel occasionally, are the chief
delinquents to be dealt with in particular.   Others
which fall victims to the wiles not placed precisely for
their capture must be regarded as "fair game" for the
trapper.

Hawks—to take the various species en bloc—are captured comparatively easily, but, of course, the prohibi-
tion of the use of the so-called pole-trap has rendered
such more difficult by limiting the scope of the means
at the disposal of the trapper.   It was for the purpose
of employment upon the tops of posts and rails that the
round or hawk trap was devised originally, but the
abuses associated with its use in this respect bordered
at times upon the shameful, although, properly worked
and in the hands of considerate and careful men, there
was little to object to.   These round traps can still be
employed in a variety of positions where the ordinary
type of trap would prove inconvenient or quite impracticable : but, upon the whole, the 5in. Dorset trap is the
best to use.

Taking the sparrow or pigeon hawk (the latter is
much the better name) as typical of the others, we find
it a wary bird when working in and about the haunts
of men ; but, once the human element is conspicuous by
its absence, it is a daring and fearless hunter after its

prey, quartering likely areas of ground and beating the woods and coverts where promise of quarry exists in quite regular manner. This trait is not unusual in the case of other hawks, and, as a rule, evidence of their depredations in any particular place may be relied upon as pointing to their coming again.

Fig. 31.

HAWK TRAP.

It is for the most part certain that if baits be used— and you cannot do without them very well—the hawk will be taken by the legs, unless a large trap be used, large enough to secure it round the body and cause immediate death. It is therefore advisable to err upon the size of largeness when selecting the traps to be used. The fact that in the case of round traps the jaws strike

higher up than with others is a recommendation, and
where hawks abound I should employ a specially-made
type of trap with high oval jaws and of somewhat
lighter construction than the ordinary run of large
round traps. The class of trap is shown in Fig. 31,
which exhibits its action upon the hawk when caught.
The illustration is of one fitted with a perching bar instead of a treadle. These larger traps can, in fact, be
made with bar or treadle, or a fork upon which the bait
can be impaled in attractive fashion. The use of those
with a perching bar would now be restricted to very
small limits, but occasionally they may serve a purpose.

As regards the baits to be employed for hawks, it is
only necessary to look around for the remains of what
they have destroyed to be guided correctly. The pigeon-
hawk is a particular enemy of the woodpigeon and other
wild pigeons or doves, and the partly-eaten and mauled
carcase of one, in the consumption of which the vermin
has been disturbed, is an attractive bait, as are equally
well the bodies of such birds if shot or caught and
treated as if they had just been handled by a hawk.
The same remarks apply to other victims of the hawks,
such as mature or immature game-birds or moor and
water fowl. In any case, such a bait requires to be
pegged down where it may be discovered, or in such
place chosen for its disposal for the purpose in view.
The trap must be set where the hawk is likely to attack
the bait. In such a case it does not stoop and seize the
bait with its talons, but alights possibly a yard or more
away, and, approaching it, will then take hold and
proceed to tear the flesh with its beak. Occasionally,
however, the hawk may perch upon a convenient bough

and then drop on to the bait with its talons, intending to remove it. In any case, the result should be the same, as the trap, placed at the most convenient point for the bird's approach, is almost certain to secure it.

When trapping for hawks in a general way, and without reference to any particular act of destruction, it is necessary to select sites for the baited traps where the presence of such bait is not unlikely, and where it may be as conspicuous as possible. You may frequently see sparrow-hawks alight upon any small mounds there may be in the pastures, such as old and over-grown mole-heaps, the large heaps of earth thrown out by rabbits from surface burrows, any large protruding stones or rocks, and so forth. These always prove more or less fatal spots for these hawks when a trap carefully set and covered and judiciously baited is placed upon them. The bait most likely to attract is a quite young rabbit, immature game-bird, thrush, blackbird, or the like. The bait must be placed in crouching position, such as is assumed by the bird or animal when a hawk is flying overhead, and be attached to the treadle-bar or fork of the trap, otherwise in stooping at it the bait may be taken and the vermin escape.

The work of the sparrow-hawk in covert is carried on in somewhat different fashion. To those acquainted with the habits of these birds, the peculiar gliding motion they pursue as they thread the rides and paths in almost silent manner is well known, as is also the quartering they do above the trees, dropping into any openings between, where their prey may be obtainable. Similar tactics as regards the disposal of traps and the baits to be employed can be pursued here with equal success. A good deal of the trapping done for other winged vermin serves also against the sparrow-hawk, notably as regards immature game losses through their malpractices; but, with what has been set forth to serve as a basis, other opportunities and other means will suggest themselves as they occur.

It is impossible to ignore the kestrel as an object of the trapper's art, because at times—notably when rearing its young—it is very destructive among poultry and young game, acting with a recklessness and daring wholly foreign to it at other times. The means for checking these depredations are similar to those employed for the sparrow-hawk, and as the kestrel is very persistent in its ways at such times, it is not difficult to capture.

There is a plan for taking hawks when the young are being reared which will usually succeed when all others fail. It is necessary, however, to secure the young from the nest—a matter easily to be accomplished when the old ones are otherwise quite unapproachable. Before the young are taken, prepare a small piece of fine-mesh wire-netting, about 18in. square, by forcing it into the form of a small dome. Peg the sides down in a clear place easily discernible from the kestrel's nest, and place one or two traps alongside. As soon as the young are obtained, put them beneath the dome of wire-netting, and within an hour or so you will have one or both parent birds.

As regards other hawks upon moorland, common, and fen, practically the same principles of trapping for them are brought to bear as already described, differing only in the baits employed and the sites chosen for the

traps. As a rule, however, general, as opposed to particular, trapping will have to be practised more largely.
Hawks working over such large areas do not return so
frequently to the same expanses of ground; consequently the fact of a grouse killed here, or a leveret
there, and only partially consumed, is not so sure an
indication of the return of the vermin at an early moment. It may be that the delinquent will return, but
it may not; however, the bait may serve for others, and
should be utilised as already directed.

AN OLD OFFENDER.

CHAPTER XV.

TRAPPING CROWS, ROOKS, ETC.

The class of predatory birds of the crow tribe proper includes the raven, hooded and carrion crows, the rook, and the jackdaw, but it will be mainly with the two species of crows and the rook (at times) that the trapper in these islands will be concerned.

The raven is to only a small extent obnoxious to the preserver, and occasionally the shepherd in some of the wilder parts of the land, and, owing to steady decline in numbers, is more often protected than destroyed. They are difficult to trap, and, with the exception of a variation in the bait, the mode of placing traps for them is similar to that for carrion or hooded crows.

The rook is associated with the crow because, whatever may be its value in other directions, certain members of the tribe not inconsiderable in number pursue precisely similar practices as the crows, and, as far as egg-eating is concerned, largely excel them. The jackdaw is also at times extremely destructive, but it is only exceptionally that it has to be trapped for specially, and for the most part it is when associated with others of the Corvidæ that it falls a victim to the trapper's art.

No two birds are so regularly and universally confounded as the carrion crow and the rook. The name "crow" is applied indifferently to both, and it is probable that a very small percentage of those directly interested in them can distinguish one from the other at sight, despite the marked feature of the discoloured bill and bare face of the rook in its second year. To the close observer, however, the dissimilarity is sufficiently marked to tell them, even in flight, one from another. The rook is a slimmer looking bird, has a less laborious-looking flight, and an entirely different manner of movement when upon the ground. Then, again, the rook is essentially gregarious, whilst the crow is equally solitary, but in pairs.

It may sound paradoxical, but it is true that where crows are most plentiful they are most difficult to catch. They are most easily accounted for where they are of comparatively occasional occurrence. The trapper constantly on the lookout for objects of his craft will discover the presence of carrion crows or proof of their misdeeds; despoiled nests of small birds, rabbits mature and immature, killed and partly eaten, fair-sized leverets (the back portion over the kidneys is the favourite part), young game-birds, and frequently mature partridges, grouse, and black-game, and occasionally pheasants. Young wild duck are peculiarly liable to attack, and the denizens of poultry-yard and pen equally so. A curious trait in connection with these birds is that they will attack the carcases of ground vermin, stoats, weasels, rats, and hedgehogs, which have been killed, coming to them on repeated occasions when disturbed. I have no knowledge of them attacking or killing them when alive, though they may do so, but I doubt it seriously. The rook, upon the other hand, never does this. The crow will "go for" stoat, weasel, or hedgehog killed in a trap, and I have over and over again taken pairs of these winged vermin with such as bait, but notably with stoats. I daresay vermin trappers have often remarked that the bodies of stoats, etc., have been attacked and torn, and wondered what had done the injury; it would be carrion crows.

The crow—carrion or hooded—is a far more artful customer in its method of working than the rook, and in watching it you may be perfectly sure that it never goes directly to its prey. It will view it out at a distance and then manœuvre so as to drop on it suddenly. Thus: A young rabbit out feeding in solitary satisfaction will be spotted by a passing crow; it pursues its way, turns, comes back on the opposite side of the hedgerow, clump of brake, or well in and above the tree-tops if near a wood, pops over or drops down, as the case may be "from nowhere," a vicious peck at the eye, the brain is struck, and the victim smothered in a very few seconds. Similar tactics pervade its every action when in quest. It may or may not consume its prey then; it may carry some off to its young in season, or hide the quarry or the remainder away to return to later. In any case, the crow is sure to come back and the discovery of the body of its victims or partly despoiled nest or brood is half-way to capture of the marauder and its mate.

Any trap of fair size, 3in. to 4in. jaws, will serve to catch crows, but choose the type according to the position where it will be placed. This will be decided according to the direction in which it is presumed the crow will approach the bait. Reasonably close covering is required. Any bait placed in the open will require a trap upon each side, possibly three, as the crow will walk round and round perhaps several times before deciding to take hold, and is as likely as not to do so from the least expected point.

In many portions of the country the carrion crow is only an occasional visitor. A pair or a few pairs of them will make their appearance, and if you can account for them by trapping or otherwise no more may be seen for a month or so more. On the other hand, there are districts where crows are always present in more or less numbers, and it is necessary to be always on the look-out and prepared for them. General trapping then comes in, and the manner in which it must be worked depends upon the nature and manner of the crow's depredations. Grouse moors suffer more probably than any other class of preserve from the inroads of these vermin, whether of the hooded or common variety, and almost every kind of available bait likely to prove attractive is employed to bring them into the traps, offal and carrion being used to supplement any such as the bodies of dead game may afford. The crow is naturally of an inquisitive turn of mind, and will visit all sorts of odd corners, where traps thus baited are set, so much so that the mere presence and passing of the trapper over the moor will not infrequently cause them to follow in his tracks.

It is obviously impossible to enumerate all the possible likely places for traps; they should suggest themselves as they occur, but very often passing crows may be drawn to where the traps are placed by a scattering of clean sheeps' wool or of light-coloured feathers, according to circumstances, round about where the traps are set. Upon closely-preserved partridge manors or pheasant domains the general trapping of crows will be effected by traps placed for magpies and jays, and the one description of the modus operandi will serve for all.

Where the rook follows in the crow's footsteps as far as furred or feathered game, mature or immature, is concerned, precisely similar means to compass its destruction must be taken. It is, however, chiefly as an egg-eater and destroyer that the rook proves most obnoxious and injurious when it takes to the practice. More persistent or wholesale work in this respect no birds are capable of than the rook once it adapts egg-eating as a means of livelihood, and the trapper will often have his work cut out to secure the offenders. All rooks do not do it, but the disease appears catching, and once you find one or more at it you are sure to discover many eventually if the vermin be not cleared off. Pheasants and partridges are the chief sufferers, and it is remarkable how, once the taste is acquired, rooks will ferret out the best hidden nests and raid them. You can always tell the rook's handiwork in this direction. A half-destroyed nest will show a few untouched in the nid, and a small stream of broken and sucked ones leading from it. The rook drives its beak into the egg to start with, and thus lifts it from its nest. It keeps dipping into it, and as the contents become exhausted it further breaks and rolls the egg away from the nest until its every contents is cleaned out. The vermin will return again and again until every egg is eaten, and if disturbed, or for other reason, they will take a half-eaten one in the beak and carry it away in flight.

Of course, if you discover a half-despoiled nest, you have the best possible lure for the vermin, and ordinary traps, or those of the round or light steel pattern, can be

put down at once with almost certainty of securing the
rook or rooks responsible for the spoliation. If, however, the nest be wholly cleaned out, the shells remaining serve to assist in forming dummy nests as lures.   In
any case, when trapping egg-eating rooks, a supply of
mock pheasant and partridge eggs should be on hand,
and with a few of these— five or seven to make a show—
as the nucleus of the nest and a few of the shells of real
ones in which some of the contents of fowls' eggs should
be disposed, the means are available for making up the
whole appearance of a partly raided nest.   Choose as
site a place likely to be one where either of these game-
birds nest, but so situated that side-approach is impracticable.   You will often find such in a bunch of briars
or between two such bushes, under gorse, or in like
places.   Two, or even three, traps may be necessary,
and the egg-shells and traps should be so disposed as to
provide for the taking of the vermin as it attacks the
shells in the one case, or the mock eggs in the other.
As a rule, a single egg is a poor bait for a rook, but two
or three serve the purpose very fairly.

The traps should be of fairly large size, and must
be carefully concealed.   For the rest, the taking of the
rook of predatory habits in a general way is similar to
that of magpie or jay, and will be referred to further
when we come to deal with them.

CHAPTER XVI.

TRAPPING MAGPIES AND JAYS.

There is little necessity to insist upon the mischievous nature of these two birds, and the persistency with which they exercise their predatory instincts. The malpractices of the two are mainly of similar character, and it is not unusual to associate them closely in this respect; but the intelligent observer soon learns to discriminate between the work of the two species and the characteristics which mark their individual destructiveness.

There is no period of the year when magpies and jays offer less difficulty in trapping than during their nesting and rearing season. As soon as ever the young are hatched, the incessant calls for food which they make upon the old ones cause the latter to forego much of the wariness they exercise as a rule, and as soon as the young leave the nests they also are comparatively easily taken—a fact largely due to their innate inquisitiveness and curiosity. It is chiefly amongst the eggs and young of all game-birds in particular, and many others in general, that the destructive nature of these two birds asserts itself. I think, upon the whole, that the magpie does more damage in coverts, upon commons and moorland, than does the jay, which works mostly along hedges and hedgerows, in small coverts and spinneys, and along the outside of them. The jay

is more akin, as far as dietary goes, to the rook, and
the magpie to the crow; but both are persistent egg-
eaters and dreadfully destructive amongst immature
ground and feathered game.   The magpie is more
easily kept down in its numbers than the jay, due
mainly, I think, to the more easily discoverable and
accessible nest which it builds.   Constant persecution,
too, will cause, the remaining individuals of a tribe of
magpies to clear out and find other quarters, whilst
jays do not appear to be influenced similarly.

Both magpies and jays constitute themselves the
natural sentinels of the woods and other parts which
they frequent, and the trapper in search of suitable
positions for his traps, etc., will have occasion to
learn and distinguish their cries, which, uttered as
notes of warning and alarm, may, if followed, lead him
far from their regular haunts, and he may find himself
setting for them in places which they least frequent.
They are both difficult birds to take, except at the nesting season, and, were it not for their persistently inquisitive nature, they would be still more so.   They are
extremely wary, and it is no easy matter to get even
with them.   When trapping for them, a 3in. Dorset
type of trap is a fairly useful one for working with;
but the light steel traps of American pattern referred to
already are very effective.   If, however, working with
eggs or other small bait, a 4in. trap is necessary, as the
vermin must be taken by the head.   Speaking generally, larger traps are required for magpies than jays;
the latter can very frequently be taken in small traps
placed in positions in hedgerows where a larger-sized
one would be impracticable.   In judging as to the

places where to trap, you will do more service by observing these birds from a distance and then putting
down traps where you have seen them frequenting. It
is impossible to enumerate and give precise details of
all the possibly favourable sites. Watch the vermin,
locate the particular spots they frequent, and then
search out evidence of their depredations.

Probably the best baits are immature rabbits or portions of larger ones. The eye or eyes, apparently a
tit-bit, will always be pecked out first; then the vermin
disembowels its victim and consumes the kidney and
portions of the back parts, eventually consuming most
of the flesh, but always working from the inner side of
the skin. The neck and shoulders are also laid bare,
frequently, and consumed. If a small rabbit be employed as bait, open it up and expose the inner flesh.
A small stick, sharpened at both ends and thrust into
the skin one side, passed round the back, and fixed in
on the other, does this well. Use two traps—one
against the head and neck, the other where the body is
opened. Where portions of a larger rabbit are used,
paunch it and tear it up, so that the fur adheres to the
several portions provided. Expose the flesh and peg
it down, using one or two traps as the conditions demand. Similar handling should be applied to the
bodies of dead birds, game or otherwise, which may
come to be employed. It is not necessary that they be
specially killed for the purpose; any young game-birds
which may be picked up, or weakly or dead chickens,
serve the purpose of baits for both birds. A dead mole
or hedgehog with the abdomen ripped open is a good
bait, and mice or small rats tied to the plates of the

traps, the latter being set and well covered, often prove effective. It is unwise to be sparing of traps when dealing with these birds at baits pegged down, as you cannot be sure from which point the vermin will attack the bait.

The magpie if disturbed is almost sure to return to the prey it was disturbed at; but the jay is more likely not to do so. There is a manner of taking magpies when the young first fly which I have found frequently very successful. First locate them on the tops of the trees, where they will be; then go and dig up with your trapping tool a round space of new ground about a foot or fifteen inches in diameter. Here set and carefully cover a large-sized trap and leave it. Probably before you are a couple of hundred yards away you will have effected a capture. Watch from a distance, and as soon as you succeed repeat the process. I have frequently taken four or five young magpies in succession at the same place when trapping in this manner.

Jays which frequent the hedgerows, the outskirts of coverts, small clumps of trees and individual ones, employing either place as a centre of operations, as it were, may be secured, as a rule, by employing a young rabbit as bait to two carefully-covered traps placed on each side of it. Along hedgerows the lure can be repeated with advantage about every 50 to 70 yards. It is chiefly along old hedgerows, honeycombed with rabbit burrowings, that jays work, and also those with a close top-growth of hazel, etc., where they easily conceal themselves and pass from place to place without being observed. They are particularly disposed to frequent and hunt about young plantations divided by drives and paths, and also along similar places in covert, and here again the small rabbit as bait is a good one. You will also be able to take them with the small steel traps set upon the branches of oak and ash at such places where the formation renders it possible to place them close to the stem. The branches from about nine to fifteen feet above the ground are the most likely ones

I have left the matter of taking magpies and jays with eggs as bait until now, as it is a manner of doing so which if practised properly is very effective, but if mismanaged entails a lot of trouble to no purpose. It must be remembered that egg-eating birds such as magpies and jays (as well as rooks and crows) possess a singular facility for moving them which it is not usual to credit them with. Thus you will often find the bait gone or interfered with without the trap being sprung. It is rarely that, having discovered one or more eggs, the vermin seeks to secure its booty right away. For many reasons, then, it is frequently more effective if one or more of the shells put down as bait be filled with clay, or, what is better, plaster of Paris (which does not discolour the egg), in which a pointed stick of two or three inches length is firmly embedded. Thus provided, the egg or eggs can be made a fixture, and the vermin caused to manœuvre round it, and so probably get into the traps; otherwise it will probably reach to the eggs and lightly draw one towards itself, or by a sharp, jerky push roll it away. The process may be repeated until the bait is a yard or more from the trap, when, of course, the time and trouble employed in setting are lost

I dealt with the matter of nest-despoiling when treating of rooks and crows, and the same mode of trapping is applicable to magpies and jays when on similar intent. Single eggs are not very effective baits for the former, but they serve very well for the latter. Small white hens' eggs from bantams or other small fowls serve the best purpose, single game eggs being of little use. They are best placed in such spots where semi-concealment is possible, such as under thin brambles in the approach to a gap in a fence or hedgerow, so that their presence in an unlikely spot is not made too glaring. When using ordinary traps, eggs provided as above can be fixed in position, and the traps—3in. are large enough—be set and neatly covered, on both sides if practicable. When the egg is placed as bait upon the treadle of the traps—4in. or larger in this case—it should be sufficiently broken at one side so as to lie firmly on the treadle; so that if the vermin try to draw or push it off, sufficient force may be exerted to spring the trap. Of course, if it drive its beak into the egg to start with, as rooks and crows mostly do, so much the better.

With a view to obviating this pushing away or drawing off of the egg, and thus rendering the trapper's efforts nugatory, and still to ensure the effective working of the trap, Henry Lane has quite recently brought out a new trap, of which an illustration is given at Fig. 32. By an ingenious reversal of the action of tongue and treadle, the trap is caused to act by the mere withdrawal of the egg employed as bait. Instead of the usual treadle, a ring is provided upon which the egg is poised. So long as it remains there, the trap is inactive, but if it be lifted or rolled off, the trap acts instantly, and the quarry is secured by head or neck. The mechanism is very simple and sensitive, and there is no fear of "sticking" as is the case in traps built with the usual action applied to "hugger" traps. The

Fig. 32.

TRAP FOR EGG EATING BIRDS.

trap is easily set and held safe by one hand whilst the egg is placed in position by the other; but I would recommend caution to those unaccustomed to the use of traps with reverse action, otherwise fingers are liable to suffer. When setting the trap, which should be placed, if possible, where grass or moss covering can be employed, I have found it best to employ a large pocket-knife to keep the trap set pending the placing of the egg in position. I slip the open blade through

the ring, and the weight of the handle, acting as a
lever, keeps it in position. Then, when the trap is
covered and ready, I place the egg in position and
gently withdraw the knife-blade.

The traps are naturally of fair size, but can be placed
in a position where other forms of trap would go, especially the ordinary round ones, and should do very well
in deserted nests. I have tried them for rats as well,
when these vermin are taking eggs, and find they serve
equally well in such cases—altogether a very valuable
and useful addition to the trapper's armoury.

A final word or two upon the subject of taking magpies and jays in general may prove useful. Although
so wary and sometimes cunning, it is almost invariably
the case that where you succeed in taking one of these
vermin you will capture others also. The fact of one
or more of their kind getting into trouble does not seem
to alarm the remainder, and the adage that one crow
does not peck out another's eyes is by no means generally correct. I have on several occasions known magpies "go for" others of their kind when caught in
traps. It is, however, well to remove all signs of a
capture, feathers, etc., before resetting the trap or
traps, although the same bait and position may serve.
Magpies will frequently attack rabbits caught in traps,
and generally kill them through the eyes when they do
so. In such a case the rabbit may be left as it is to
serve as bait, and, if you chance to be troubled in this
way, it is a good plan to kill and leave in the traps a
rabbit here and there where the birds are likely to prove
troublesome. Jays occasionally offend in the same
manner, and may be taken similarly. You will also

sometimes find jays caught in traps set for rabbits—
right in the burrows at times.   What takes them there
is doubtful, but maybe they "sound" the burrows for
young rabbits on the move.

CLEVERLY CAUGHT.

CHAPTER XVII.

BOX, CAGE, AND OTHER TRAPS.

There exists quite an array of specially constructed traps which may prove serviceable from time to time for taking all the furred and some of the feathered creatures to which reference has been made already. They are in the nature of permanent traps, i.e., traps that can be put down or prepared and remain always set and ready for work. For the most part they are designed to take the quarry alive, but some in which the principle of the dead-fall is embodied kill the victim when it is caught. Several types of these traps can be bought ready-made, the only fault to be found with them being that too much or too expensive work is put into them, so that their employment in any number becomes rather a serious item of expenditure. So long as the traps work well and serve their purpose, there appears to be no necessity for elaborate or costly workmanship in their construction. If by employing a home-made article the price can be reduced by about one-half or more, there is every reason to be satisfied with the more roughly and cheaply made one. I propose, therefore, to supply dimensions and instructions for making some of the more effective of these traps.

The principle upon which all box or cage traps should work is one in which the movement of a treadle by the quarry insures its capture. Some work with baits, and some without, but in any case the effectiveness of the trap must be reduced if seizure of the bait is necessary to provoke its action. There are several ways of applying the principle of a movable treadle to box and cage traps by which the shutter or flap at one end or both ends is caused to fall, thus securing the animal which throws off the trap. I shall describe these methods and their application in turn. Meantime, at Fig. 33 is shown the simple form of box-trap. This is made of ¾in. deal, and should be fastened together with brass screws or copper nails, to prevent the rust which ordinary nails or screws would soon cause, to the detriment of the trap. Reference to the sketch will show the trap to be provided with a grating of iron rods at one end and a shutter (which must work freely in grooves) at the other. The action is quite simple, the trigger and treadle working through a slot in the roof of the trap being hinged on a small brass rod held in position by two similar staples, driven into the top of the trap upon each side of the slot, giving lateral play. The catch can be adjusted to work either way, as shown by lateral movement or, reversed, by downward pressure. Upon the top is an aperture covered with a small sheet of zinc, to which the bait, which hangs downwards in the trap, is attached. The trigger is of iron, the treadle of zinc. It is suggested not infrequently that these traps are just as good without the barred end, but the contrary is the case, and, except by the merest fluke, nothing is likely to enter them. Unless the animal can see right through, it will not enter. The fact that it cannot pass right through is not so material a factor in regard to the likelihood of captures being made. The dimensions given in the sketch are large enough for poaching cats, polecats, or foxes (in districts where they can be caught legitimately), and will serve equally well for stoats or rats.

The trap as figured can be constructed—if a number be made at one time—at a cost of about 3s. 6d. each,

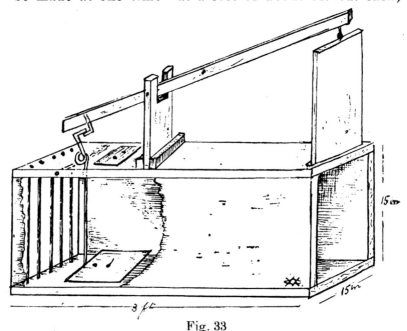

Fig. 33

ORDINARY FORM OF BOX TRAP.

with the fittings as described. Any country black-smith can rough out the bars, treadles, etc., and the lengths of rough-planed wood can be obtained to order cut to measurements. There is then very little trouble in fitting them together. When traps of this description are made of different dimensions, it will be found necessary to vary them relatively; thus, for stoats, rats, and weasels, 2ft. to 2ft. 6in. in length by 6in. square, outside measurements, will be found the most suitable ones. For large poaching dogs they must be correspondingly increased in height and width as compared with the length.

Double-ended traps working upon this principle— i.e., box-traps with shutters at both ends which drop and close simultaneously—have to be constructed upon a slightly different principle, and with quite another form of treadle. Two standards in which the arms supporting the shutters are suspended are necessary, and the arms cross one another at their extremities over the centre of the trap, and are held in the depressed position they occupy when it is set by a length of thick picture wire fastened to one side of the trap, passing over them and working at the trigger on the other. In the bottom of the trap at its centre a moving wooden treadle is fixed working on pivots. This treadle is flush with the bottom of the trap, but works easily in its position. One pivot protrudes at the trigger side of the trap, and is square-headed outside the level of the trap. Upon this square portion a piece of stiff iron or zinc sheet about 1-16in. thick by 1¼in. wide is firmly fixed.

At Fig. 34 I give a detailed sketch of the treadle, trigger, etc., which shows the treadle working in the base of the trap. A is the piece of stiff iron or zinc fixed to the square head of the pivot; B is a piece of bell-spring strongly nailed to the side of the trap at D. E is a piece of brass attached to the wire G, and F F are two zinc pins driven into the side of the trap. The sketch shows the trap when set, the wire holding the arms down, leaving the shutters at each end raised and

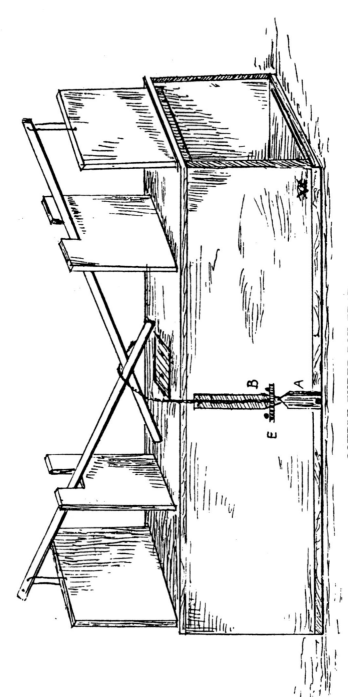

DOUBLE-ENDED BOX-TRAP.

open. Any animal attempting to pass through depresses one side of the treadle, the tongue A is moved to one side, the end of the spring B flies outward, releasing the trigger E, the wire is released, and the trap acts, both shutters falling instantly and securing the capture.

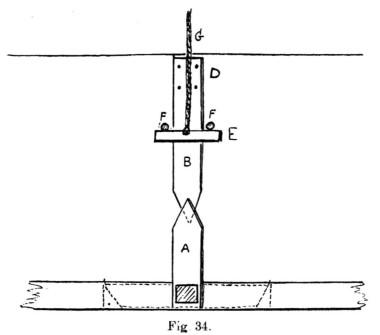

Fig. 34.

TRIGGER FOR DOUBLE-ENDED BOX TRAP.

The bait is hung in the centre of the trap in the manner shown in Fig. 33.

These traps are rather more expensive to make than the ordinary box-trap previously figured, but they are more effective, as they exhibit a clear and apparently safe run through. Their length must, of course, be greater in comparison with their breadth and height also than the first one, so as to obviate too great a lever-age of the arms carrying the shutters.

When making these box-traps, ample margin must be allowed for free working of treadles, doors, etc., otherwise they are liable to stick in damp or wet weather.

The principle of the dead-fall can be applied effec-tively to box-traps, and, where it is desirable or imma-

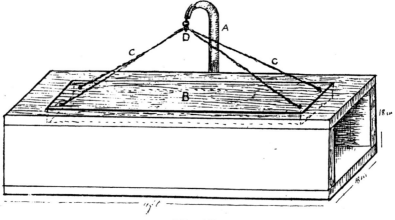

Fig. 35.

OPEN-ENDED DEAD-FALL TRAP.

terial that the quarry should be killed when captured, traps so fitted are to be preferred to others. In these dead-falls the attempted passage of the animal to be caught over the treadle releases a sufficiently heavy weight which crushes and kills the victim. Box-traps working upon this principle are more easily constructed than those already described. The trigger and treadle arrangement are the same as shown at Fig. 34; but, as will be seen from the sketch at Fig. 35, the box is open-ended, and, instead of shutter-doors falling, a portion of the top of the box which is held in position by wires is released and descends into the body of the trap.

The stanchion A is of hollow rim-iron (such as is employed for small wheels carrying a rubber tyre), flattened where it is fixed on to the box beneath the bell-spring piece of the trigger arrangement (see **Fig.** 34). The dead-fall B is of heavy wood, thick slate, or other material, or wood carrying weights, and should just occupy the space cut out in the top of the box to receive it. C C are supporting wires—six-ply copper is best—attached to the trigger wire at D. The trigger wire is shown in the sketch ready for action, which results immediately the treadle is depressed, from whichever side the victim enters. Of course, when constructing these traps, the working parts must be accommodated to the weight of the dead-fall, but the **length of the treadle should not be unduly increased, otherwise** the animal entering will throw the trap before it is sufficiently far under the fall. The size of trap illustrated —viz., 4ft. by 18in. square—is full large for ordinary poaching cats, but is equally effective for much smaller vermin. Dead-falls will often take the former if the inside be tainted with valerian, but it is just as well **to** employ small baits, such as liver, fixed in the dead-fall as in the box-trap, to attract other animals.

The dead-fall traps, besides costing less than the box-traps to construct, are frequently much more successful, especially for polecats where these creatures are at all plentiful. The best positions for them are in gaps and gateways where vermin are likely to run, and in dry water-courses where they pass under hedgerows, walls, etc.

Various types of box-trap of different construction to those I have described are obtainable from various makers; but, as I said before, the cost of them much militates against their employment in large quantities. Some, however, are really very effective, and, being so well constructed, stand long and rough usage—facts which render their acquirement by no means unprofit-

Fig. 36.

TUNNEL-TRAP.

able. At Fig. 36 is given an illustration of a tunnel-trap for small vermin—rats, stoats, weasels, etc.—which is both cheap and effective. It works with a bait inside and a treadle to throw it, and, being of small size, is safe as regards dogs and winged game. Of course, the capture is killed instantly when caught, but a similarly working trap provided with spring doors which close at each end and take the animal alive can be obtained. Its construction is more elaborate, however, and the cost correspondingly dearer.

At Fig. 37 is an illustration of another form of box-trap, which can be employed for taking either small furred or feathered vermin alive. The system upon which it works is clear enough without detailed de-. scription, but it may be mentioned that it works either

Fig. 37.

ANOTHER FORM OF BOX-TRAP.

with baits or by means of a mirror at the back, which attracts the intended capture, and the latter, depressing the treadle, throws the trap, and the lid (which is fore-shortened in the illustration) closes upon it. Made in large sizes, these traps will take poaching cats or can be utilised for catching up pheasants and partridges. It provides a useful auxiliary to the other box-traps, at times, and the cost is not excessive. Curiously enough, this trap is a clever adaptation of a very old form of what were called chest-traps about a century ago, and were then the only form of box-trap available for the purpose, and required considerable ingenuity in the construction.

I do not think any good purpose would be served by referring in detail to any of the other forms of box-trap; the working principles are the same—it is the form of construction alone which varies. I shall therefore pass on to the matter of cage traps.

Cage traps may be of various patterns, but they are for the most part constructed of wire-work, and, consequently, more easily purchased than constructed at home, although, where wood is employed, this is a comparatively easy matter. They secure the quarry alive, and, being easily portable, can be changed from one position to another without much trouble, their weight being much less than the wooden box-traps. Small vermin, poaching cats, etc., appear to enter cage-traps with much less suspicion than they do the ordinary box-traps, probably on account of the fact that most birds and animals do not appear to grasp the fact that wire-netting or wirework generally is impassable, and always appear to imagine that there is a place of egress where none exists.

At Fig. 38 is a sketch of a very simple, but very effective, form of cage-trap, which I have employed for taking rats alive, and also used successfully with both stoats and weasels. Inter alia, it is a capital trap for catching up a lost ferret or one left behind in a burrow. The cage is of wire, and the door of sheet zinc, which falls by its own weight, being kept in position when down by a wire double-arm piece. It works with a bait and treadle, the quarry throwing the trap by depressing the latter to reach the former. At the back is a small entrance with a falling flap, which permits ingress but does not allow anything caught to pass out. In the case of rats, the first one caught acts as lure to others, and very effectively so. I have several times had

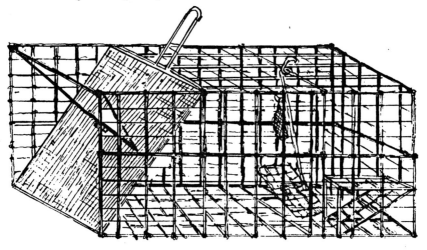

Fig. 38.

SIMPLE CAGE-TRAP.

three, four, and even five rats in one of these traps. They are purchasable through almost any ironmonger or dealer in such articles. The same principle can be applied to box-traps made upon these lines, but the wire ones are much to be preferred.

I have had similar traps of semi-circular form in which a portion of the top slid back, working with a spiral spring, which caused it to fly down again when sprung. This pattern is also very effective, but the springs soon lose their power, and the tendency to "stick" restricts the action.

When dealing with the trapping of rats I referred to a square wire cage-trap in which a live rat played the part of lure. I give a plan, etc., of this trap at Fig. 39. It is of wire-work, 2ft. square, 6in. deep, and at the centre is a smaller compartment 9in. square, into which a small wire cage to contain the live rat as lure is placed. At b.b are the entrances, shown larger in

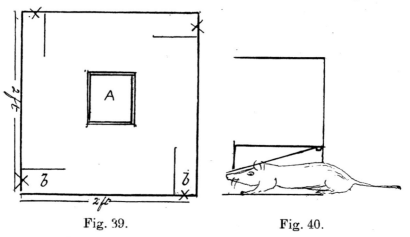

Fig. 39.   Fig. 40.

PLAN AND SECTION OF WIRE CAGE-TRAP.

section at Fig. 40. The four entrances are small tunnels fitted with a drop-down flap, which rises as the quarry pushes its way in and closes behind it. There is a door at the side for removing any animals caught when desired to have them alive, but for rats immersion in a large tub of water is the simplest manner of destroying them before removal. I have had several of these traps in use from time to time, and never known them fail in connection with rats. It is necessary to repeat that the bait-rat must be fed and provided with water what time the trap is in use.

An application of this trap to the purposes of taking stoats and weasels can be made which insures its proving effective for taking these vermin alive, which it is not when used in the ordinary way. The idea came to me in connection with an underground one for small vermin—to be described later on—and was, in fact, suggested as a less troublesome, and admittedly a less productive, substitute for the somewhat complicated one in question.

I cut out a square in the ground sufficiently large to take the cage, and deep enough to allow a two or three-inch thickness of turf covering being placed over it. Where the entrances are at the corners, I scooped out corresponding holes leading down to each of them in the form of the entrances to a rabbit burrow. The bait cage I kept supplied with fresh bait in the shape of young rabbits, small birds, and the like, tainting the entrances with a light lure. The covering over the bait cage should be loose enough to permit any passing vermin to wind it, when they find their way in at the burrow entrances and are duly taken. A wooden trap with wire entrances would serve the purpose equally well, I expect, provided it were properly seasoned inside before being put down. Naturally, the bait cage would have to be of wirework, but the inconvenience attaching to a trap of this kind in which you could not see the captives taken is also obvious.

There is a very excellent cage-trap patented by Mr. Alfred Clifford, Hawley, Kent, and supplied by him, which is upon the principle of the double-ended box-trap, but with falling doors at each end instead of shutter-doors, which are released when the treadle in the floor is depressed from either side.   Sizes to suit small vermin, poaching cats, or foxes are obtainable, and those who have used these traps speak very highly of them.   They are well made and not expensive in view of the good work put into their manufacture.

The device which I am now about to describe is in

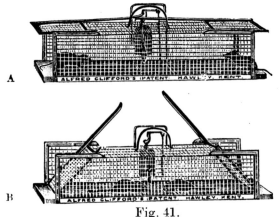

Fig. 41.

A, the trap set; B, the trap sprung.

ALFRED CLIFFORD'S CAGE-TRAP.

the nature of a pit-trap, or, rather, a combination of traps, and was the invention of or originally described by "Idstone," years ago.   It is in the nature of a permanent trap, as, once prepared, it only requires occasional attention to insure its remaining in working order as long as you choose to maintain it.   A suitable site must be chosen where there is old close pasture or moss-ridden grass and a pit excavated.   First the turf is carefully removed to a depth of about three inches, and then a square chamber formed not less than 3ft.

square and from at least 15in. to 2ft. deep, according to
its area. A wooden cover of 2in. deal, or, preferably,
1½in. elm, must be made, having an aperture in the
centre at least 18in. square, with corresponding lid.
At two or more corners of the pit entrances must be
made as shown in Fig. 42. They must be from 3in. to
4in. in diameter and slope down from the surface like
the entrance to a rabbit burrow. There is an easy way
of forming them. Obtain a piece of willow of the
necessary size and length—say, 4ft. by 4in., and

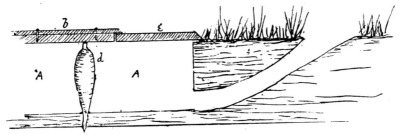

Fig. 42.

A A, square of pit ; b, opening and lid in cover ; e, cover to pit.

SECTION OF "IDSTONE" PIT-TRAP.

slightly curved. Across the flat of one end nail a cross-
piece 1ft. long. Then with a narrow spade—"draft"
is the technical term for it—dig out a sloping channel
to the required depth, after having turned the turf
back in the direction required. Then lay your willow
piece in the channel so that one end protrudes into the
chamber, and fill in the soil on top, treading it heavily
down, but working the wood from side to side by twisting the cross-piece. Then, when it is ready, withdraw
the timber, and the small artificial burrow will remain
taut and trim upon the inside.

Now prepare a spindle as shown at d, and drive it firmly into the ground until its upper end is on a level with the cover. Then set and tie open four Dorset traps—Lane's collapsible traps cannot be beaten for the purpose—and dispose them as shown in **Fig. 43.** Do not use a long chain, but peg them down with an iron

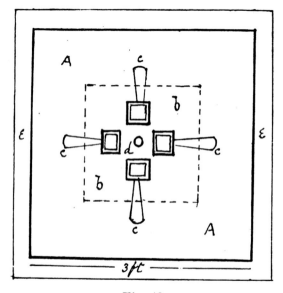

Fig. 43.

A A, square of pit; b b, opening in cover; c c, Dorset traps; e e, square of cover.

PLAN OF "IDSTONE" PIT-TRAP.

stake attached to an S-hook fixed on the traps. Obtain two or three small birds or young rabbits, which kill and place in the trap-pit. Cover it over and place the turf removed over the cover. Visit the trap in two or three days and see if the baits have been taken away; if not, wait another two or three days till the vermin have found out your lures. As soon as they do, renew the supply, and when this again is taken set the traps carefully. It is not necessary to cover them, but this may be done if preferred. The great point is to make sure that the stoats, weasels, or rats, as the case may be, are regularly "running" the trap before commencing to catch them, because the fact that one or more are secured will have little or no influence upon the others, and it is by no means unusual when working this contrivance to have a capture in each of the four traps at one time. The pit-trap should be visited every morning to remove anything caught, and fresh bait supplied from time to time until it fails to attract. Then tie down the traps again and feed as before, thus preparing for a second campaign.

Wherever stoats, weasels, and rats abound in woodlands, brakes, and the like, one of these "Idstone" traps should be prepared. Once the vermin find it out and "run" freely, it is surprising how effective they are. I had one placed—one of the first I ever made—in a corner of a plantation, about 15 yards out from the corner. There were two gateways in the opposite hedgerows fitted with poles to lift out, as there was a pathway through this corner. It was a favourable position, and within about three weeks I took upwards of sixty head of various vermin in the one trap-pit. From this it is easy to know the class of site to choose for this arrangement. They may be placed in any suitable spots within or without a covert, but not in situations where horses or cattle are likely to pass, as such knock the whole thing to pieces. If any trap-pits are going to be formed, it is better to provide separate

coverings for each, and not necessarily remove the
covers from those temporarily ineffective. The latter
can then be left for a time and be made ship-shape
again when required for further use.

It is curious to note in connection with this trap-pit
that "Idstone," although referring to and praising it
in his writings on game preserving, left the scantiest
description and roughest plan possible of his idea,
which I had in my possession for some years before I

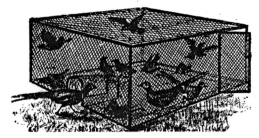

Fig. 44.

TUNNEL CAGE-TRAP.

could make head or tail of them. I may therefore,
with all diffidence, claim to having resurrected this
scheme of trapping.

There are only one or two other forms of cage-trap to
receive consideration, and then we are done with this
portion of the subject. The most practical form of the
true cage-trap is that in which a tunnel or funnel provides the means of ingress, from which fact these traps
are classed generally as tunnel traps. They are manufactured in various forms for taking either birds or
furred creatures, but the principle remains the same.
I give an illustration of a very useful form at Fig. 44,
which shows one of a size large enough to catch up

pheasants, and serves equally well for such birds as wood and other pigeons. I have also taken both jays and magpies in these traps, but it is necessary to place one or more live members of both of these species within the cage before others of the tribe will enter.

Tunnel cage-traps upon this principle can be employed advantageously for all kinds of small vermin, which enter them freely when suitable baits are provided or when others are already in them. For such, a wirework bottom is necessary and provided, otherwise, if not speedily released, the vermin burrow their way out. These cages, which are manufactured by Boulton and Paul, Norwich, are collapsible, and, therefore, very portable.

At Fig. 45 is given a plan of what may be described as a pen-trap. Devised originally by the writer for catching up pheasants, I have employed it since for taking almost every kind of bird capable of being lured into such a contrivance. This pen-trap consists of a pen with semi-open ends made of wire-netting of suitable mesh, attached to a light framework of wood or iron rod. The relative measurements for one large enough for pheasants are: Sides and top, 6ft. by 3ft. Three standards are required upon each side, 4ft. long, of which 1ft. has to be driven into the ground. The wire-netting should be laced on to the framework, consisting, besides the uprights, of two rods, 6ft. long. The wire-netting of the sides extends 18in. beyond the two standards at each end, and is laced together, from the top downwards, for about one foot of its width. The overlapping ends are bent inwards as shown in the plan —the dotted lines indicate the lacing—and form the en-

M

trances, sufficiently wide to permit the ingress of the
birds designed to be caught, but preventing egress
once the birds are within the pen.

Made in this manner, this pen-trap folds flat, and is
easily portable from place to place. The curious feature of it is that birds once within it do not appear able
to find their way out again, even if small enough to pass

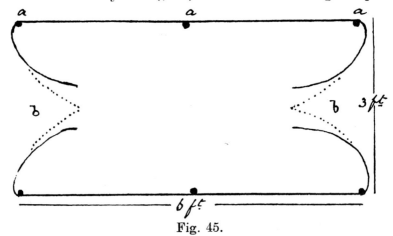

Fig. 45.

a a a, side standard; b b, entrances.

PLAN OF PEN TRAP.

between the sides of the entrances. It is one of the
best traps that exist for woodpigeons, using corn strewn
within as bait, and small scatterings of it outside to
lure the birds to the entrances. Small pieces of rabbit
flesh, raw and chopped finely, serve for magpies, crows,
and jays.

For ground vermin it is also applicable, but the ends
require drawing together so as to compel the vermin
to push through, and, as it can be set up anywhere considered likely to prove fruitful of results, there is no
limit to its employment in many and varied directions.

CHAPTER XVIII.

THE SNARE AND ITS VARIETIES.

Since the passing of the Ground Game Act the snare has again come into far greater use than was the case for some years previously, when it shared with the steel trap that general use which the Act in question denies to the latter. As a matter of fact, the snare in one form or another has been an engine of universal employment for taking almost every description of "bird and beast of chase and venerie" since time immemorial, and is so used to-day by those adept in handling it. As far as "fur" is considered, it is mainly employed in the British Isles to-day for taking hares and rabbits legally and illicitly, and also, in the form better known as hingles, for almost every kind of bird which may figure as an object of the modern fowler's art. Except in the case of ground game, an enormous amount of illegal snaring and hingling goes on all over the country, and, as far as modern gamekeepers are concerned, it would be very much better if they were more fully acquainted with all the ins and outs of the business, as they would then be far better fitted to detect practices which go on without their knowledge or discovery.

There is not the slightest doubt that the snare in skilful hands is a most effective, and at the same time simple, contrivance, whilst the opportunities for its application are infinitely more numerous than are those of the steel trap. Its cost is extremely small, and by a multiplication of the numbers used it can be made to be effective over a much larger area.

I shall pursue the same course as regards the snare as was followed in the case of the steel trap, viz., take the snaring of rabbits as the basis of instruction as to the making and using of this "engine," and then proceed to the consideration of its varieties and their application under varying conditions. The simple form of snare is usually made of a length of several-ply copper wire or picture-hanging wire formed into a noose and attached to a length of cord or twine, which in its turn is fastened to a stake driven into the ground. The wire to be employed should always be of six-ply and all copper. "Coppered" wire—i.e., steel wire coppered over—will not serve the purpose. As to thickness of the six-ply, that depends upon the gauge of wire used, but should be about the thickness of the thinnest size of knitting needle. I put it in general terms because the gauges of wire are known and understood by few of the people who deal in it in retail. The length of each strand of wire for the snare must be 22in. to 24in., never less, for rabbits. The advantage of buying the wire in six-ply form is apparent in the greater ease it affords for fashioning the loops necessary at the end. These small loops must be from ¼in. to ½in. in diameter, and are best formed by tying a bow-line knot or by splicing, if you are adept at either practice; otherwise form the eyes by tying a double knot at the end. This will involve from 2in. to 4in. of the wire respectively, according to which method of forming the eye is employed, and leave, accordingly, 20in. or 22in. length. At the other extreme end of the wire tie a single knot to prevent unravelling. Now take an 18in. length of stout whip-cord or other twine or cord which will not kink when wet. At one end tie a single knot to correspond with the one on the wire. Then tie the two together by tying each one round the other and drawing the two tight. This will give a compact and trustworthy join.

The stakes should be made in the same manner as those recommended for traps, with a hole bored through them 2in. from the top. To attach the cord of the snare to the stake pass the end through the hole, make a complete circle with it round the stake, and bring it back again through the hole, taking a half-hitch round the cord with the end of it. Of course, the loop of the snare must be completed first by passing the end of the cord, etc., through the eyelet at the end of the wire. A possible improvement is to add a small, simple swivel in between the cord and wire; this is a matter of individual choice or fancy. For each snare a small hazel peg 12in. long, ¼in. in diameter, sharpened at one end, and cleft at the other is necessary.

At Fig. 46 is a rough sketch of an ordinary rabbit snare set as it should be in a rabbit-run, the noose being poised between the flattened spaces where the rabbit places its feet, as it is at this point that the rabbit is taken. At B and C are details of the knots recommended to be used when making the snares. To tie the bowline forming the eyelet at the end of the snare take the wire near one extremity between the thumb and first finger of the left hand, forming a small loop which

is held fast, leaving the end portion free and lying next
to the finger. With the right-hand thread the loose
end through the loop, round the wire beneath it, and
back again, following the lines as shown at B. Then
pull it tight and the eyelet is formed, with no possible

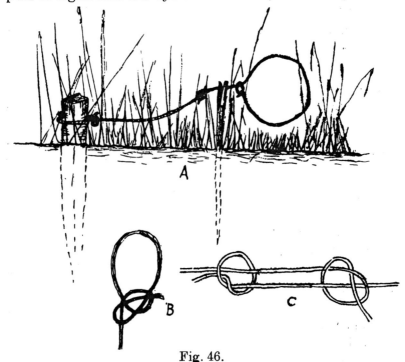

Fig. 46.

A, the snare; B, bowline knot; C, angler's knot.

ORDINARY RABBIT SNARE.

chance of its coming undone. The details given at C
of what is generally called the angler's knot, which is
employed to join the cord and wire, are self-explanatory.

In connection with the stakes employed for snares, it
is necessary to point out that they must not be driven

in too deeply, a fair length of the top being left out of
the ground to be grasped when they are withdrawn.
When moving snares the trapping hammer should be
carried so as to be available for loosening the soil
around them when necessary.

Personally, I do not think it possible to improve upon
the snare and mode of fashioning it as here described,
modified in size and strength or increased according to
the quarry to be taken. I see nothing gained by buying thin wire and plying it yourself when what is manufactured is infinitely superior and costs no more. It
is quite as easy to verify the quality of the one as the
other, and whenever a large number of snares have to
be made at one time a reduction in their cost is assured
by purchasing in quantities. One particular point to
be observed is that the nooses of the snares when placed
in position shall not sag or lose their form, whilst another is that the wire be held tight in the peg, so that
it shall not be influenced by the shrinkage of the cord
attachment caused by damp, dew, or rain.

Besides the supply of complete snares provided with
stakes, a further quantity will be necessary for attaching to any boughs, branches, or standards of under-
wood or hedge-growth which may be immediately available. As a rule, the practice is to tie such to the particular piece of growth which may be on hand, but a
better plan is to increase the length of the cord portion
of the snare sufficiently to admit of a loop being formed
at its end, through which the remainder of the snare
has been passed after taking it round whatever it is
made fast to, and so avoid the trouble of tying and un-
tying, and often cutting.

Those who prefer to purchase their snares ready-made can be supplied by nearly every purveyor of sporting goods at prices according to the value of the material worked into them. At Fig. 47 is given an illustration of a very effective snare as manufactured and sold with all appurtenances ready for laying. Amongst other

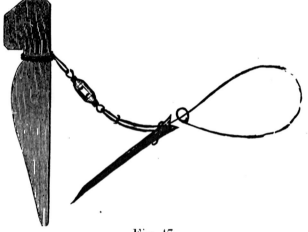

Fig. 47.

AN EFFECTIVE RABBIT SNARE.

forms recently placed upon the market is one in which the principle of the springe is worked in, so that, directly the rabbit is caught, full tension is put upon the noose, and the animal is speedily suffocated. It has, however, little to recommend it over the ordinary snare properly worked, but I shall refer to it in further detail when dealing with the springe in general.

CHAPTER XIX.

THE USE OF THE SNARE.

Speaking generally, the snare is employed for taking ground game under very similar conditions to those applying to the use of the steel trap. In dealing with the latter I made no reference to the taking of hares with it, as I regard its employment for this purpose as quite unwarranted, even if possible, under conditions other than those set up under the Ground Game Act. Where hares have to be caught, the snare is infinitely to be preferred. A larger and stronger form of the one already described is necessary for the purpose, but otherwise no difference in the make of it is required.

When dealing with rabbits it is mainly, but not entirely, upon the more or less well-marked runs that the sites for placing the snares must be selected. I have already described, under the trapping headings, how to distinguish between well-worked and neglected runs; but, when snaring, those must be selected which indicate that the rabbit has a free run over them, and not those where the quarry is likely to dodge about in its course. To this end those will have to be selected rather distant from, or well clear of, the hedgerows whence they emanate. As a rule, more execution will be done from ten to twenty yards out from the burrows or lying ground, if under low cover, than closely adjacent to them. Then there will be other cross runs or runs lying irregularly parallel to the hedgerows or cover, which will also prove fruitful of results. As before mentioned, the rabbit must be snared as it rises from one leap or falls to the following one, thus necessitating the placing of the snare between the foot-places of the rabbits and over the unpressed grass or ground in between them. The height of the bottom of the loop of the snare should be about a hand's-breadth above the solid surface of the ground when the snare is placed in position, and advantage should always be taken of any possible covering growth to hide the sides of the loop and the remainder of the snare. Upon the other hand, care should be exercised to disturb the growth, etc., alongside the runs as little as possible, and not to draw any extraneous matter up to them for disguising the whereabouts of the snare. Upon straightaway runs it is not likely that the snares will be brushed aside without effecting a capture, but when snares are placed nearer to burrows or hedgerows it frequently happens that this is the case, though it may very well be for no fault in the manner of laying them.

It is a common error amongst those employing snares that the rabbits can see the snares, and another that they cannot do so. As a matter of fact, both ideas are incorrect. The rabbit may see the snare when nearly abreast of it—it is likely to do so in certain phases of moonlight nights when some distance off—but, as a rule, in the open runs the rabbit rarely sees it till too late for its safety. This applies to those snares placed in the runs upon which the rabbits may be moving in fairly rapid to full course; under other circumstances

they are very likely to see them unless carefully concealed, as.far as such be possible.

Wherever surface rabbit burrows exist, it is little use
putting snares down near the actual holes, as they are
either brushed aside or else the capture of a rabbit by
one renders the others useless by scaring the remaining
rabbits.   The runs leading from the burrows are the
proper sites, and also those leading to any "scrapes"
worked by the rabbits from the particular burrows.
Runs through gaps, gateways, and the like are usually
fruitful of success, snares to be placed upon either side
of them.   In woodlands many places will suggest themselves, but, as I said before, the sites for laying the
snares should always be chosen where the rabbits have
a free run.

The best time for putting down snares is the forenoon
of the day, earlier or later according to the time of year
—earlier when the days are short, later when long.
Snares may also be laid in the afternoon, but the morning ones always make the larger percentage of catches.
Remember also that rabbits almost invariably leave
their burrows down-wind, and let this fact be a guide as
to where most of the snares should be placed.   The
quantity of snares to be put down should be regulated
by the approximate number of rabbits available for
catching.   Thus, if by careful observation you have
made out that a certain hedgerow burrow contains about
a dozen rabbits, put down equal to half as many again
the number of snares, doubling them on the main runs
at twenty yards apart, and dividing them on the two
sides of the hedgerow according to the force and direction of the wind or the attraction which the food available provides.

It may be generally taken for granted that it requires three snares to be put down for each rabbit caught, and the fewer the rabbits the greater the quantity of snares necessary to insure the taking of them. Three day and nights' snaring is sufficient at a time for each set of snares to be down at one place, and when they are moved it is as well to follow the same course as that recommended for traps, viz., to so arrange matters that the successive settings overlap one another. It will be the case, as a rule, that wherever rabbits are concerned their workings will be in series or groups, and endeavour must be made to encompass, as it were, each group with an entourage of snares, and so make each successive operation as complete in itself as possible Where the snaring is more or less disconnected, this, of course, is impossible, but endeavour should be made to make the work as comprehensive as possible. It must be remembered that with snares you are bound to miss a considerable percentage of the rabbits expected to be caught, so that endeavour should be made to provide for many more than will actually be caught. It is only in this way that you can hope to make snaring as thoroughly effective as trapping, where rabbits are concerned.

Snares intended for taking hares require to be made both larger and stronger than those for rabbits. Thicker wire, thicker cord, and longer stakes are necessary. Hares vary in size according to districts, and snares intended for them should be two-thirds as large or as large again as for their smaller congeners, as far as the wire and loop are concerned, but it is not usually necessary to increase the length of cord. The setting is practically the same, but, to judge the distance of the bottom of the loop, add the height of the thumb extended upward to that of the average hand's-breadth.

The hare's mode of progression differs somewhat from that of the rabbit. In slow course it is almost identical, but in full course it lies down much more to its work; in other words, it extends itself much more, with the result that a hare suddenly pushed up or in full course may run under a snare placed at the full elevation, or brush it aside. Thus it occurs that the actual taking of a hare in a snare is not very difficult, whilst, on the other hand, the correct choice of sites for hare snares is a more difficult matter. It is no truism to assert that the habits and movements of the hare are but imperfectly known to the generality of those whose duty or pleasure it is to snare them legitimately, and before you can make any hand of this part of the art of how to trap and snare you must acquaint yourself intimately with the movements day by day, or rather night by night, and hour by hour of the hare itself.

It is impossible within the present limits to more than hint at the nature and scope of the hare's run. Its form is not difficult to discover, and there is always a run or sort of run by which it approaches it, but the hare is in the habit of leaping to one side to break its tracks, so that it is necessary to provide such form-runs with more than one snare, distant only ten to fifteen yards apart. Then, again, the hare forms at a distance from its feeding-grounds for the most part, and pursues an irregular path in passing from one to the other; but there will always be certain stretches of ground, more or less extended, which it invariably follows. These will be situated where it passes from one field to another, from pasture into woodland, through gaps or gateways or over watercourses, where it crosses roads or, maybe, bypaths, rides, and the like. It is only rarely that one hare regularly uses the runs of another, but occasions do arise where such is the case.

Regular woodland hares—i.e., hares which form in the woods, as opposed to those which frequent them only occasionally, follow well-marked runs more than the latter-named of the two kinds, and, as a rule, are more easily taken. These hares for the most part feed outside the coverts they affect, and their comings and goings always follow one or perhaps more defined routes from their form to the place or places where they leave the covert. Moorland hares are more erratic, but mostly observe certain defined runs.

In any case the trapper must, by careful observation, in the first instance discover the regular as opposed to the irregular movements of the hares he wishes to capture by snaring, and locate his snares accordingly. This class of ground game feeds mainly from dusk to daylight, and their movements at other times are not to be relied upon as an index of what they will be during the darker hours. According to what is certain, so the snarer of hares must elaborate his plans. As a general rule, one or two snares are sufficient to put down for each hare tried for. If you have determined correctly the movements of the quarry, there is little difficulty in securing it at the first attempt.

Snares of a smaller and lighter kind can be employed for taking a large variety of small animals and birds.

Naturally, the snares require to be made on different lines. There are two equally good methods for making these small snares, either with wire or with horse-hair. In the former instance very fine copper wire is employed, and the manner of forming the actual snare noose is as follows:—Take a 2ft. length of the wire, double it, secure the loose ends in a small vice, and, employing a piece of rounded wood ¼in. in diameter, place the latter through the looped end. Then, using the right hand to twist this round, and the left to regulate the twisting, continue the process until the whole of the wire is firmly and regularly twisted up. It is important that the wire be evenly and regularly twisted, otherwise it will kink in the setting. Then release the ends from the vice, tie them in a single knot, and thread them through the eyelet formed at the other end, thus forming the snare. A length of gimp or whipcord completes it.

When using horsehair, a similar length is employed, doubled in similar fashion, and then twisted up from end to end, the portion retained between the thumb and finger at the first twisting providing the eyelet. A knot at the loose end prevents the hair unravelling and being passed through the eyelet completes the little snare. Gimp or picture-wire of suitable size finishes the article.

Small wire snares of the former description can be employed for taking rats in almost any situation where it is impracticable to use traps. Such opportunities occur mostly about buildings, outhouses, etc., where rats have their runs and holes through the woodwork and floorings. I have also employed them upon narrow

rafters and beams where rats run, and at their holes
where there are workings in banks and hedgerows, also
around stacks. The snare should be placed so that the
noose of it lies just against the aperture or entrance to
the rats' run, and forms a circle from 1¼in. to 1¾in. in
diameter, according to the size of the hole it is placed
against. If the hole be a small one, then the noose of
the snare should be a shade smaller still, but if the aperture be large, then the limit of 1¾in. must be employed.
If a larger one be put down, the rat may get one or more
of its forelegs through, with the result that it will be
enabled to bite through the snare and escape. When
using snares for rats, something in the nature of a
peg is required to hold the snare in position. Small
hazel twigs will serve out of doors, but where the surface is wood, as in and about buildings, etc., whether
hazel or suitably formed wire supporting pegs are used,
a gimlet or bradawl is necessary to make holes in which
they can be fixed.

The small horsehair snares may be employed for taking various birds of predatory habits, such as magpies,
jays, and hawks, at nesting-time. Magpies are fairly
easily taken on account of the form of the nest, as the
opening at one side frequently offers good opportunities
for taking them. Laid in the nests of jays or sparrow-
hawks, where accessible, they also prove useful at times.
The manner of working them otherwise, more as hingles, comes, however, under the heading of general
snaring, and will be dealt with subsequently.

Large and strong snares are very useful at times for
taking poaching cats and dogs. You will not infrequently find that the latter particularly and the former

also, but less regularly, may leave coverts and woodlands where they have been working by pushing through or under gates, gaps, and the like. Evidence of the fact is generally forthcoming from the stray hairs attaching to bush, briar, or woodwork where the creatures creep or push through. For poaching cats a hare-snare is sufficiently strong, but for poaching dogs still stronger ones are necessary, made with wire of larger gauge and closely twisted, as this prevents the noose sliding back when the animal is caught, and is more speedily effective. It is possible to fix up box-traps with a noose inside and a spring-hazel outside, so that when taken the animal is automatically hanged; but the arrangement is not wholly to be recommended.

Of course, snares are employed illicitly much more largely than otherwise, but I do not propose to produce a manual for the poacher, and shall not do more than refer to the fact.

CHAPTER XX.

GENERAL TRAPPING AND SNARING.

DEADFALLS.

We now pass to what is practically an entirely different style of trapping, snaring, etc., in which what may be described as old-fashioned methods almost entirely predominate. The fact that they are old-fashioned does not in the least detract from their utility. Indeed, it would be an end greatly to be desired that the army of gamekeepers and vermin-catchers of the present day were more conversant with these methods than is actually the case. In practically every instance the "engines" employed are home-made, and require a certain amount of care and ingenuity in their construction, but they are not costly, are very effective, and can be employed in many situations and under many circumstances where the ordinary run of manufactured steel and other traps cannot be utilised.

These various methods may be divided into three classes, namely, the use of the principle of the deadfall and pitfall, the use of the springe, and the use of the hingle. In the former the trigger arrangement is such that when sprung a weight or cage descends and kills or captures the quarry, as the case may be; the pitfall is self-explanatory. The springe consists of a pliant stick to which a noose is attached, so that when the quarry is secured the springe flies up and holds the quarry caught and suspended. The hingle is an application of the snare to work upon the surface of the ground, by which the quarry is secured by the feet.

In nearly all forms of the deadfall the trigger which releases the weight is either a figure-of-four one or based upon that principle, and I shall therefore in the first instance supply the necessary instructions as to how to

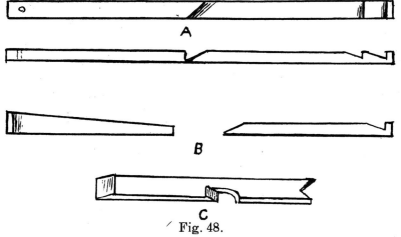

Fig. 48.

A, stretcher; B, slanting stick; C, upright.

PARTS OF FIGURE-OF-FOUR.

make this figure-of-four in the easiest and most effective manner. It is made out of three pieces of wood cut and shaped to size and of relative proportions, which, fitted together, form a "4." Reference to the illustrations at Fig. 48 will show how these are cut so as to secure firmness of fixture when set up, and immediate collapse when the bait is touched. It is necessary to remark that care must be observed in cutting the slants and notches correctly, otherwise the 4 will not prove trustworthy. When making any quantity of these

triggers, I have always had the various pieces cut out
truly by a carpenter, a dozen or so of each at a time, in
well-seasoned deal, planed, and then cut in the slants
and notches myself, finally staining them with umber.

The measurements which follow are of a size of trigger adapted to stoats, weasels, or rats. The parts can
be made relatively larger or smaller to fit the 4 for
other quarry. The stretcher A is 14in. long, ½in. wide,
and ⅜in. thick, with three notches cut as shown—two
at the end, square across, and one at the centre, diagonally. Their depth need not be more than ⅛in., but cut
them slightly inclining inwards, so as to give a firm
grip. B is the slanting piece, 7in. long, ⅜in. wide at
the smaller end, increasing to 1in. wide at the larger.
at which it is notched, the former extremity being
slanted off sufficiently to fit comfortably into the notches
on the stretcher. C is the upright, 8in. over all, 3½in.
from the forked end to the notch. It is also slanted at
the other end. To cut this notch correctly, place the
upright, which should be 1½in. wide and ¾in. thick, on
its side, and make a straight cut half through with a
fine tenon saw ; then, using a sharp knife, cut the slant
on one side and the curved notch on the other. The
forked cut in the end is to prevent slipping, and a hole
in the extremity of the stretcher renders easy the attachment of a bait.

The simple form of deadfall, or, as it is now more
frequently called, the "figure-of-four trap," involves
the employment of a slab of stone or slate 18in. by 12in.
in size, to fit the measurements given, or a similar piece
of boarding with two or three strips of wood nailed

across the top to retain any stones or other weights placed upon it.

At Fig. 49 is a sketch of the trap when set. To effect this first fix up the bait, whatever it may be, upon the lower side of the stretcher. The bait must always be something of a soft character—liver, lights, etc. Then place the cover or dead-weight in such position as it would occupy when fallen. Raise one end, and, using the left hand and wrist to support it, place the

Fig. 49.

FIGURE-OF-FOUR TRAP (SET).

upright in position at one-third the length of the stretcher from the end of it. Adjust the slanting stick with the right hand, and you will have the weight of the cover on its extremity above the upright, thus releasing the left hand with which to put the stretcher in position. Carefully feel whether all the notches, etc., bite, and, this being the case, gently release the hold; the 4 will then be formed and in position. The slightest pull at the bait or touch of the end of the stretcher releases the trigger, the whole thing collapses, and the weighted cover falls, crushing the bird or animal beneath it. The action of this deadfall is almost instantaneous, and it is rarely that it misses a capture when fairly thrown off.

The figure-of-four may be employed in a variety of ways for other forms of fall, such as those made in the form of a square basket reversed, or of laths of wood built up in pyramidal form. These will take the quarry alive, and are very useful for catching up old single cock pheasants, bachelor partridges, and the like. Any worker in wicker will make the former at quite reasonable prices, and the latter can be put together out of hazel sticks, round or split, or other similar material which may be available. When employing the last-named, the best way to go to work is, having obtained all the wood required, to set up four pieces for the uprights, of a length according to the size of cage or fall required.

Drive four pieces about six inches into the ground, at equal distances apart, at the corners of a square; then bend the other ends towards the centre and tie them all together. Nail, or fix with wire run through holes and twisted up tightly, four stoutish pieces round the bottom, and continue the process with shorter lengths at intervals of one, two, or three inches until nearly to the top, when the remainder of the side uprights are cut off and an aperture is left large enough through which to remove the bird or animal caught. This is closed by a flat stone or weighted board so as to maintain the fall in position when it is down. Another mode is to nail the pieces one upon the other, commencing with a square of fairly short willow or hazel pieces, then, using smaller ones, of gradually reducing length, build up a square cage of pyramidal form like the other one.

At Fig. 50 is given an illustration of the wicker-cage deadfall, but a different form of trigger to that of the figure-of-four is shown. This trigger consists of a bent wand known as the bender, which is fixed into the wickerwork at one side so as to be a couple of inches off the ground, and a couple of small sticks about 9in. and 6in., respectively. In the centre of the former is a

Fig. 50.

WICKER-CAGE DEADFALL.

slight notch, and the latter is flattened at one end and slightly pointed at the other. To fix the trigger the longer stick is placed against the bottom of the wicker at one end, and the other poised against the bender; the smaller stick is stuck firmly on the ground, and the flat end fixed in the notch of the longer one. In this manner the front of the cage is held up until anything presses on the bender, when the trigger collapses and the cage falls. The same trigger can be adapted to the deadfall first described by nailing the ends to the sides

of the board-covering and bringing the bowed portion of
the bender to the front of it.

I have made a sketch at Fig. 51 of a deadfall in
which either a whole log of timber or one sawn in two
pieces lengthwise provides the deadfall, and a number of
short stakes driven into the ground protecting or guid·
ing sides. Worked with a figure-of-four trigger, this
form of deadfall is actually very deadly. It can be

Fig. 51.
DEADFALL OF TIMBER.

made in sizes to suit various kinds of quarry, from
poaching dogs to stoats and weasels, and, although in-
volving some little labour in the preparation of the
timber and the setting up, they last for a long time,
and are always ready for use when required. I had
quite a considerable number of these set up in various
favourable sites in the woods of a West-country manor,
rebaiting them from time to time and renewing the triggers when necessary, with the result that they accounted for quite a formidable array of both furred
and feathered quarry when ordinary traps proved stale
and unprofitable.

CHAPTER XXI.

PITFALLS.

The pitfall was probably the first form of trap ever devised by man, and its employment to-day cannot be ignored altogether. The form of pitfall of most value nowadays consists of a wooden frame, poised within the limits of which is a lid or covering, which, fixed upon pivots, gives at once to any weight imposed upon it, and allows the latter to drop into a pit or cavity previously prepared beneath it.

At Fig. 52 is an illustration giving the section of a pitfall suitable for taking ground vermin—stoats, weasels, and hedgehogs—alive, or for securing rabbits in similar manner. It consists of an outer framework, 5ft. by 4ft. by 2in., within which is poised a cover 3ft. by 2ft. by 2in., or less; but with easily working pivots 2in. is not too thick for the cover. The latter at the inner ends is bevelled off, as will be seen, to admit of free working. Upon each side of the cover a circular hollow is cut out and lined with suitable pieces of brass; corresponding circular pieces of the same metal provide the pivots, and a small metal or wooden flap working on a screw serves to cover the working parts upon each side. Should the cover not lie evenly when fixed, a small disc of lead nailed beneath the lighter side will serve to regulate matters. A pit of suitable size and depth is dug, and the cover, etc., are properly adjusted

over it, as shown.   Some light covering may be shaken
over the pitfall at first, but as soon as the woodwork is
weathered a little this may be dispensed with.

To attract rabbits to it, place a small heap or ridge of
wood-ashes across the centre of the cover, renewing
them from time to time as they become moist or wet;
whilst for small ground vermin employ any likely bait,
but draw some gorse or other suitable bushes or briars
up to each side, so as to prevent the vermin from at-

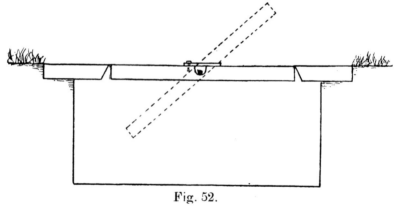

Fig. 52.

SECTION OF PITFALL.

Showing working of Cover and manner of fixing.

tempting to reach the bait from the sides, and not the
ends.

A few of these pitfalls may be formed at any likely
and suitable places for the purposes intended, but they
cannot be employed where cattle roam about, and I
always make a practice of putting up a notice to warn
persons of the fact, as they are rather dangerous to limb
when concealed from view.   It is also necessary to remember that pitfalls, when in working order, should

be visited every day in the case of those put down for
rabbits, or else some form of food should be placed in
them, otherwise any captives will be starved to death.
In the case of furred vermin a dead rabbit should be
left in the pit unless daily visits be made.

It is possible to construct a simple form of pitfall out
of any suitable form of barrel by utilising the end pieces
as the lid, working upon pivots. Barrels thus provided
are effective for taking rats in buildings, or, if a barrel
be cut in two, the two halves can be partly or wholly
sunk to act as pitfalls.

CHAPTER XXII.

SPRINGES AND HINGLES.

To be precise, it must be stated that most springes comprehend a hingle in their composition. Hingles are small snares or nooses made of horsehair, fine gimp, whipcord, or wire. I have already (see under "Snares") described how these small horse-hair, etc., hingles are made, and there is no necessity to repeat the instructions. For most purposes twisted horsehair is strong enough, but, plaited threefold or doubly twisted in fourfold, it will hold a pheasant or a hawk.

Springes are useful in a great variety of ways, but, unfortunately, we must go to the poaching fraternity if we wish to see them put to the fullest use. The same may be said of the simple hingles. Inasmuch, however, as they may be employed to take anything from a rabbit to a mouse, or from a pheasant to a snipe, the usefulness of these old-fashioned "engines" is obvious. The present generation of gamekeepers, vermin-catchers, etc., possesses very little knowledge of these matters, and those slightly interested in trapping and snaring know probably—with few exceptions—nothing at all about them. However, I trust from the descriptions and sketches which follow that they will be able to understand, make, and use them.

The ordinary springe consists of a bent rod A (vide

Fig. 53), thrust into the ground, to the extremity of which is attached a length of whipcord. At the end of this is a small cross-piece b (see Fig. 54), 2½in. long, shaped off at one end to a somewhat obtuse flat point. C represents a small crook-stick 6in. in length, which is driven into the ground so as to leave ¾in. between the surface and the under portion of the crook. The latter, as will be seen, is bevelled off from the upper side, so as to leave again ¾in. upon the under side. To the lower

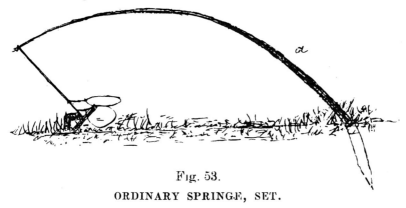

Fig. 53.
ORDINARY SPRINGE, SET.

end of the whipcord attach one or two horsehair hingles. To do this effectively, the whipcord should be opened in its twists, and the end of the hingle threaded through. This will maintain the latter in its proper position, and also afford sufficient support for it. I have drawn Fig. 54 so as to show the actual setting of the trigger of the springe, but the position of the hingles is somewhat out of drawing, so as to make the matter clearer. The dimensions here given are those applicable to birds such as starlings. They must be relatively increased for larger birds, such as pigeons or

winged vermin. The bow or bent rod may be from
2ft. 6in. to 4ft. or more, according to circumstances,
and is best made of hazel, although holly or sallow will
serve the same purpose.

When working with these springes it is a very good
plan to carry a short stick, shod with a sharp-pointed

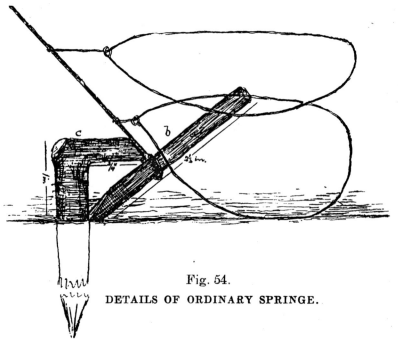

Fig. 54.

DETAILS OF ORDINARY SPRINGE.

ferrule, and carrying a good crook handle. It is for
placing over the bow when bent, whilst the hingles are
being adjusted. The setting is simple enough, but the
crook stick is useful for preventing the bow springing
up and tearing out the hingles, etc. The action of the
springe is very quick and simple: a bird hopping or
trying to perch upon the cross stick, or pushing against

it, instantly releases it, and, the bent rod flying up, the bird is secured by the feet or neck, as the case may be.

Fig. 55 shows another form of this engine, known as the bow-springe, which is useful in many directions where the ordinary one is not applicable. It consists of three pieces, a complete bow formed by fixing the two sharpened ends of a hazel stick in the ground, an upright (b), and a cross-piece with a fork (c). The bow

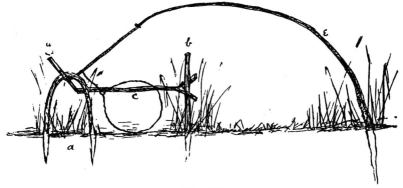

Fig. 55.

BOW SPRINGE.

and upright are placed so much apart as the length of the forked stick may determine.

To set this springe the bow is pulled down, and the end of the cross-piece (d) poised against the plain end of the fork-stick (c), which in its turn is poised against the upright (b). The bent rod (e) can be fixed to work from either end, and the noose adjusted as shown, or be laid over the cross-piece for birds hopping on to or perching upon it. The value of this kind of springe is due to the fact that it can be set at almost any distance, close to or above the ground, and in such manner that

it is thrown off either by an animal or bird brushing
aside the cross-piece, or, as already mentioned, by birds
perching.   It is necessary to point out that the sketch,

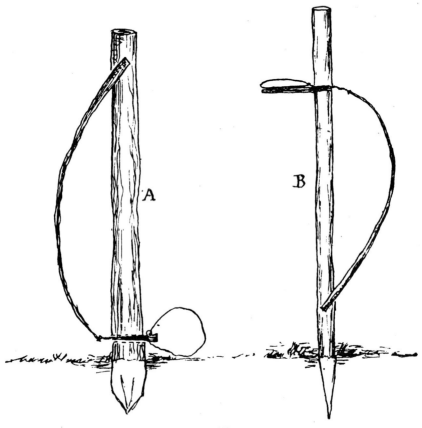

Fig. 56.

POST OR RAIL SPRINGES.

Fig. 55, is not drawn to scale, but in such a manner as
to show the working parts clearly.   The height, size,
and width of them apart will depend upon the nature

of the quarry and the manner in which it is intended that it should be caught.

To make the series of springes complete, I show at Fig. 56 two forms of it as applied to posts or rails. As will be apparent in each case, the bow is formed by fixing the thick end into a hole made by an augur in the post or rail. At the point where the noose is set, a cleanly bored hole passes completely through the post or rail. Its diameter may vary from $\frac{1}{4}$in. to $\frac{3}{4}$in., according to circumstances, and through this the noose is passed, the cord to which it is attached, and which is fixed in its turn on the bent rod, being held fast in the hole by a plug or the end of a small stick abruptly rounded off. In the case of the upright springe, B, a perching stick is employed for the purpose, the noose being fixed flat just above it. In the other post springe, A, the cord is held by a short plug around which the end of the noose is coiled by means of a half-hitch. In the latter case a furred quarry attempting to pass the hingle dislodges the plug: in the former a bird attempting to perch displaces the perching stick. In each instance the springe acts immediately.

I do not think it is necessary to go into very close details as to how and when these springes can be employed. To a large extent their use is self-explanatory in view of all that has gone before in regard to snares and traps. I will, however, mention one or two special circumstances under which they may be employed, as a guide to further application of them.

The bowspringe, Fig. 55, is very useful for taking wild duck, teal, etc., upon those small water-courses which remain open and which they frequent during hard weather. At such times they will work along quite small ditches, surface drains, and in the narrow pieces of running water in the half-frozen mires and bogs. The cross-piece in such cases may extend to even 18in., when, with the noose laid over it so that one portion hangs a little lower than the other, and with the former just high enough for the duck to pass beneath, they prove very effective.

The post-springe set to catch near the ground is a sure trap for ground vermin when engaged in what is known as "running the fences"—i.e., hunting along close wooden fencing—and, applied on a large scale, will take poaching cats in a quiet and effective manner.

The ordinary springes will take almost any bird, and I have used them extensively for golden and common plover (lapwing), employing the smaller sorts of ground-worms, chopped up, and shredded raw meat as bait.

It is with this springe and also the upright ones that most of the woodcock are taken which find their way to market. It is very easy to detect evidence of the presence of woodcock at their feeding-grounds both by the grey droppings and by their habit of turning over dead leaves, grasses, etc., which they throw to right and left as they seek their food in a straight-ahead line. The leaves, etc., are left in two little ridges with a cleared space between them, and, as no other bird feeds in this deliberate fashion, there can be no mistake in identifying their whereabouts. Having located the 'cocks' feeding-ground, the practice is to form a low barrier 1ft. to 18in. high across the place, of small branches of fir, holly, gorse, broom, ling, or the like, with openings about 6in. wide about every two yards apart. At these openings the springes are set, and, as the woodcock, following their usual beat for food, meet with the obstruction, they do not rise over it, but run to the nearest opening to pass through. As woodcock do not feed where they pass the hours of daylight, it is actually the fact that many may be taken this way without in the least affecting the number falling to the gun upon the shooting-ground.

Springes can be employed with considerable success against woodpigeons, particularly when these birds—at times they are actually vermin—attack corn and pulse fields newly sown, and at almost any other time if a little corn is used as bait. The ordinary form is the best, and if a few be put down not too closely to one another they will catch without scaring the uncaught birds away.

The upright springe I have used successfully, too, against jays both on mature trees and the smaller growth on hedgerows, which these winged vermin frequent.

Before leaving the subject of springes, a few words as to providing the material for them, and possibly the plan I have followed may serve as a guide to others to whom it may appear a troublesome and time-taking part of the business. If you start out to find a sufficiency of crooked and forked pieces, it is more than likely but few will be observed. The plan I have always followed is to carry a strong, sharp pruning-knife upon my rounds, and, whenever a suitable piece of wood for the purpose showed itself, cut it out roughly there and then, taking it home in pocket or game-bag for seasoning and correct shaping out later on in spare time. Whenever hedges, etc., are being trimmed or cut down, overhaul the brushings cut out for what is wanted. In the same way, cut out your hazel, sallow, holly, or ground ash bows whenever a favourable chance offers, and so get a store of material in the rough together. Then, when the days shorten, and the long evenings arrive, many a spare hour can be profitably employed in shaping out and fitting the parts, in making the nooses and hingles. In this way the matter becomes no longer a labour or troublesome, and in the end you will be surprised at the quantity of "engines" of the kind there will be on hand.

Simple hingles—horsehair nooses—come for employment for taking small birds mostly—starlings, blackbirds, and the like. They may be attached to a small peg in the manner of a snare, or good clay worked up with tow into balls about the size of a cricket ball, in which one end of the hingle is embedded, serve an equally good purpose. Of course, hingling plays a very large part in the poacher's itinerary, as do also the springes, but there are very many and varied opportunities for their employment without making game-birds the quarry

CHAPTER XXIII.

NETS AND THEIR EMPLOYMENT.

In the early days, before the shotgun came into use, the fowler was mainly dependent upon nets of one form or another, set up by themselves or employed in connection with trained field-dogs, for the capture of his quarry. Still, to-day nets are of great importance for fowling, and are made and employed in almost precisely the same manner as was the case in olden days. I do not propose, however, to deal very extensively with this portion of my subject, but, leaving the professional part to one side, shall give such information as may be of use to the amateur, and possibly to the gamekeeper and farmer.

The most generally useful is the clap-net, or bird-catcher's net, as it is frequently called. At Fig. 57 I provide an illustration of these nets—for the whole paraphernalia comprehends two such—as they are laid out ready for work. Reference to this will make the following description plain to the reader. The particulars given here are for a clap-net suitable for taking any small birds up to the size of a starling, but the dimensions can be increased to provide nets capable of taking pigeons, pheasants, etc., in quantities.

The nets are each 6yds. long by 2yds. wide, and made of two-thread in ¾in. or 1in. mesh. They are attached at the ends to round stakes 5ft. 6in. long, so as to insure the necessary bagging of the nets when they fall over the birds taken. If taut, the birds find their way

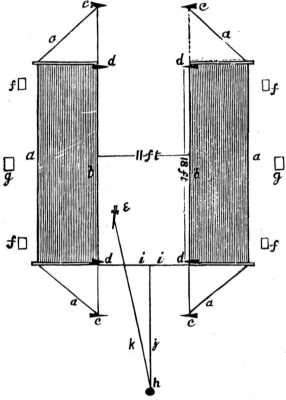

Fig. 57.

a a a, top line; b b, bottom line; c c c c, end pegs; d d d d, chief pegs; e, play-bird; f f f f, cage-birds; g g, call-birds; h, bird-catcher; i i, cross-line; j, pull-line; k, play-bird line.

BIRD-CATCHER'S OR CLAP NET (SET FOR WORK).

quickly from under them and escape. The stakes are sometimes made jointed with ferrule and cap; this is usually the case when they are of greater length. The

top line is of fairly stout, non-elastic cord, and is made
fast by a clove-hitch round the tops of the staves, leaving sufficient of the continuation at each end to make
fast to the end pegs. The bottom line is of stout whipcord similarly served. At the bottom of each stave
a cord loop is fixed to fit over the chief pegs.

To set the clap-net first extend the right-hand net in
position, as shown, then drive in the chief pegs, which
are of ash and provided with deep notches to take the
loops. The latter are then passed round them, so as to
give free play. Then drive in the end pegs and fix the
bottom and top lines to them in the manner shown.
Now turn the right-hand net over in the direction it
will lie when pulled, and lay out the left-hand one so
that it overlaps the former by six inches. Then turn it
back and adjust pegs and lines as in the former case,
seeing in each instance that the nets have free play.

Now take your cross-line of strong cord, such as
forms the top line, 25ft. in length, and make it fast
upon the tops of the two staves, having it fairly taut
between them, and to its centre attach the pull-line,
which may be of any reasonable length to suit your
purpose. The nets should now be in thorough working
order, and may be tried. For this purpose go to the
extremity of the pull-line, 30—40yds. from the nets, and
make your pull. To do this effectually hold the cord
in the left hand, so as to have it as fully taut as
possible, dropping the arm by the side and holding it
firmly there. Then extend the right arm and grasp
the line as far ahead as you comfortably can. Now
smartly and forcibly jerk—not pull, mark you—the
cord towards you until you feel the tension acute; then

release it and throw back the slack with the left. The effect of this action is to produce a double pull on the nets. The cross-cord first comes towards you and then flies inwards with a reflex action · the one raises the nets to an upright position, the other pulls them down, one overlapping the other. The whole thing is done so quickly that it must be a smart bird indeed which escapes the toils. Work your nets repeatedly to see that there is no possibility of a hitch occurring, and you can then proceed with the arrangements for bird-catching. In the case of linnets, goldfinches, and the like, two call-birds in cages are required. These call-birds are tame and good singers or twitterers. Then four cages, with birds in them which will follow the call-birds in movement and song, are required, and finally there is the play-bird.

The ordinary, callous bird-catcher is guilty of a good deal of cruelty in regard to play-birds, as not infrequent prosecutions go to show; but there is no necessity for this, and I have known a red-poll and a linnet used in successive seasons without suffering more than temporary inconvenience. The method of working the play birds is shown in Fig. 58. The peg (a) is about six inches long, with a hole bored at the top, through which the line passes, and a slot beneath for the reception of the stick. This is an ordinary piece of hazel fitting at one end into a piece of brass tubing which has been flattened near one end so as to work freely in the slot in the peg. The line is attached to the other end of the stick, and a little further along the play-bird is also attached to it by a brace (see Fig. 59). This brace is made of fine whip-

cord in which a clove-hitch is formed, and the two loops
tied together by thread or silk at a and b.   It is preferable to make the brace of fairly thick sewing silk.   The
bird is fixed in it by placing the head through one loop,
and the tail through another; the sides then fix on each
side, before and behind the wings.   The play-bird is
then fastened to the play-stick by the spare ends of the
brace, which should give it six or nine inches play.
The operation of the play-stick is simple.   A light,

Fig. 58.
a, peg; b, brass tubing; c, stick.

PLAY-BIRD FOR CLAP-NET.

smart jerk on the line throws the bird upwards, and it
then flutters down again and regains its footing.   The
action appears quite natural, and is attractive to other
birds.

Finally, the working of the clap-net is as follows :—
Having set it out as directed, with the cage and call-
birds placed near the nets, and the play-bird in position
on the left of the pull-line, some small grain and seed
is thrown down round about it and in other parts between the nets.   The bird-catcher retires to a favourable position thirty or more yards from the net, taking
advantage of any cover, such as bushes or even a hedge,
through which the lines can be carried.   Presuming

that the site chosen be a favourable one, the call-birds will attract the wild ones, and then, by judiciously working the play-bird, they are further induced to come down and feed alongside it.   As soon as the favourable moment arrives, the line is pulled, and the nets clap over the birds within their limits.

When employed for the purpose of taking other than small birds, the general mode of working the nets is

Fig. 59.

BRACE FOR PLAY-BIRD.

the same, but it is necessary that the nets should sag somewhat more for the larger quarry.

The clap-net will take starlings in large quantities, using one as a play-bird, and, by regularly feeding for them, thrushes and blackbirds can be taken.   I have used it with much success for woodpigeons, but larger and coarser tackle and good decoys are necessary.   It is best to feed the birds regularly for a day or two before making a pull.   The best time is usually very early morning.   Put down the nets over-night, and put the feed down for them at the same time.   I have personal knowledge of sixty-two being taken at one pull, the week's bag on eight pulls, morning and after-noon, totalling 240 pigeons.   The place of capture was a field of newly-sown peas.

This arrangement is useful for catching up pheasants for penning purposes, the birds being fed between the nets, and, besides this, there are many other directions in which it may be employed to advantage.

There are one or two other modes of employing nets for similar purposes to those for which the clap-net is adapted, but none of them is so effective and so portable. They are mostly in the form of drop-nets—i.e., nets suspended in some manner and dropped over the quarry when it has been lured to the ground beneath them. Inasmuch as it is much easier to put up the nets than to induce the birds to come under them, most of the skill is in the latter direction. Except in the case of pheasants which require catching up, and which for the most part will go blindly into any such trap where food is the attraction, birds require a lot of coaxing before they will go under a suspended net, and to induce them to do so it is necessary to go through a preliminary performance.

The ordinary drop-net consists of a square of twine netting tanned green or brown, either bordered with plaited tubular line or supported by a light framework. The size may vary from a few to twelve feet square. The principle is simply that of poising the outstretched net on stakes or posts, and at the critical moment releasing it by pulling a cord, the person controlling the net being hidden at a suitable distance.

For the purpose of pheasant-catching set up four standards of well-seasoned willow as straight as you can get them, or of other supple wood, about 1½in. in diameter. They must occupy a larger square at the bottom than the size of net used, but must slope inwards upon two opposite sides towards the top. At the height decided upon drive in four headless brass or copper nails, leaving about 1½in. to 2in. protruding. For the framework of the net employ bamboo poles of a diameter suitable to the size of the net, which should be spread loosely upon the framework. The net is then poised upon the four nails or pegs, and is held firmly in position by the pressure of the in-sloping standards. To the extremities of two of these, upon one of the proper sides, attach lines which come together and join to a long one leading to the place of concealment. When this line is pulled, the supports of the net come from under it on that side, while it is similarly released by the inward jerk of the supports on the other, and falls to the ground without hindrance. The pull—as in the clap-net—is a jerk, not a sustained effort.

Once the birds are under, it works well enough, but, with the exception of pheasants, it is difficult to lure them under right away. Woodpigeons and stock-doves —frequently rare despoilers of the pheasant food, besides other depredations—require, together with other birds, rooks, crows, etc., to be made free of the trap first. To this end, first feed them upon the intended site for a day or so, then set up four provisional stakes a foot or so high for a further day or two, and fix up a large bunch of furze, spruce, or holly about a foot or so from each stake, replacing the latter with the permanent ones. Then, if birds come to feed all right, put the net in position and try them for another day or so. Finally, when their confidence has been thoroughly secured, it is possible to start working the net with every chance of repcated success, because, as long as there are a few birds uncaught which have fed at the place, they will play the part of unwilling decoys for others of their kind.

Without going into further details, it will be seen that the idea of the drop-net may be applied in many directions.

The nature of tunnel-nets is implied by their name. They may be either permanent or temporary, and be of twine or wire-netting. In either case they require the support of a succession of iron rods bent to a half-hoop, or similar ones of hazel, willow, or sallow. It is usual to make these funnel-shaped, but a simple tunnel form frequently does as well, sometimes better. If the former shape be adopted, then the easiest way of shaping the netting, wire or twine, is to take a length of about 9ft. by 6ft. wide, and cut it diagonally over its length from a point 2ft. from the side at one end to another, 2ft. from the opposite side at the other end. This will give two pieces 4ft. wide at one extremity and 2ft. at the other, which, carefully laced together, provide a suitable piece to form the tunnel. When first fixed up, the two ends should be left open, evergreen branches thrown over, and food placed within the tunnel to attract the birds. As soon as they feed freely beneath the netting, close the smaller end and fix some wire-netting in the larger, in the manner shown at Fig. 60. The entrance netting must be closed at the top and arranged so that the birds push through lightly at the bottom. Of course, sparsely scattered bait must be put down leading towards the free supply within the net-trap.

Another mode of working both forms of tunnel-trap is

as follows:—Make the end hoop which supports the entrance double, leaving the rods sufficiently far apart to admit of hazel wands of the necessary thickness being

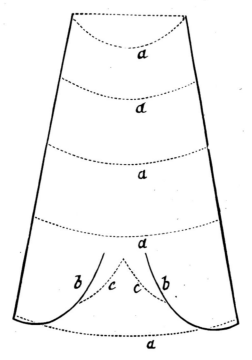

Fig. 60

a a a a, supporting hoops; b b, sides of entrance at bottom; c c, sides of entrance at top.

PLAN OF TUNNEL-TRAP.

thrust between. Choose for the purpose quickly tapering ones, and adjust them with the thin end inwards to the net, so far apart as will prevent the egress, once in, of the particular bird sought to be taken. The birds can and will push their way in, but they cannot come out.

The successful working of tunnel-nets depends upon correct coaxing or nursing of the birds before starting to trap them.

The use of the well-known sparrow and batting nets needs but a passing reference. The former consists of a long net some 6ft. to 9ft. in length by about 4ft., served on two 18ft. poles with incurving tops, hinged or looped together, the net having one or more purses at the bottom. It is worked around stacks, eaves of houses, hedgerows, and the like, the nets being folded together upon any bird or birds, which fly into them. The batting-net is a smaller one, fixed upon bowed handles, and is used in similar manner upon low hedges, ivy, etc. Both are worked at night, and, skilfully handled, are very effective.

CHAPTER XXIV.

NETS AND THEIR EMPLOYMENT (continued).

The long net is used mainly for rabbit catching. They are usually in lengths of 100yds. each, of flax or hempen twine, 2½in. mesh and 3ft. to 4ft. wide, with a long supporting line. They are usually employed at night or late in the dusk of the evening, being run out parallel with the line of hedgerow, woodland, brake, or other covert from which the rabbits come out to feed. The rabbits are then driven back by man or dog, and, becoming enveloped in its folds, are thus secured. As a rule, the net is poised at intervals upon iron or wooden stakes, hastily but carefully set up as the net is run out, but it can also be worked without by means of the line when two persons handle it. There is some art in handling the net correctly, but the main point in obtaining successful results is to get it in between the rabbits and their harbour when the greatest number are out feeding. As a rule, a properly trained dog is more effective for driving them in than the work of a man. Needless to add, this is a device largely worked by the poaching fraternity, and a very wholesale manner of rabbit catching.

At **Fig. 61** is an illustration of a more permanent form of this same device, which is very useful for sporting purposes and for getting rabbits out of land where their presence is not desired or is destructive. It is

manufactured by Messrs. Boulton and Paul, of Norwich, and the cost, considering, is not at all out of the
way. As shown in the illustrations (see also Fig. 61),
the netting is made with the lower half as a flap, which
is fixed up to let the rabbits under it, and when the
occasion arises the netting is dropped, thus excluding
them from their previous haunts. It is manufactured

 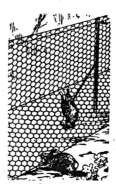

Fig. 61.

RABBIT NETTING FENCE.

(Flap up.)   (Flap down.)

in such manner that one man can drop from 100yds. to
200yds. simultaneously. Its possibilities are many,
and where rabbits are very numerous and difficult to
get at, it proves a profitable investment.

The trailing net is usually employed for catching up
partridges, but can also be employed at night for plover,
green and golden. The nets vary in size from 20yds.
by 3yds. to 50yds. by 6yds., and are leaded at the bottom. They are usually provided with a long, light
pole at each end, and are slowly trailed across field or
pasture whilst held in a sloping position. When a

P

covey or flock of birds is seen, the net is dropped and the quarry secured. Odd birds will run slowly before the net, and if the roosting places are marked down before nightfall the net can be trailed from one spot to another. Trailing nets may be employed in a number of ways for legitimate fowling, but are, unfortunately, one of the chief weapons at the disposal of poachers. Cast nets, either square or circular, are also employed for the same purpose for taking single coveys of birds.

Glade nets, usually 4ft. to 6ft. square, with "walls" 2ft. to 3ft., are used for taking hawks in covert, and also for woodcock catching. The mesh is accordingly large or small. In dealing with the trapping of sparrow-hawks, I referred to their habit of pursuing a gliding flight through rides and paths in covert, and it is when hunting in this manner that the glade nets will take them. These nets are usually served with lines at each corner of the net proper, those at the top running through small blocks, which are attached to suitable tree branches and made fast below. The "walls" are extended by twine diagonally to the square of the net. As a rule, a hawk or 'cock flying into them becomes hopelessly entangled, even when the net is fixed firmly, but it is possible to extend them in such manner as will insure them collapsing when struck.

The same principle can be employed for taking king-fishers, which, though extremely beautiful birds, are not to be tolerated in fish-rearing establishments. For these birds a very light black silk-twine net is necessary, and it is usually fixed beneath a bridge or maybe a strong plank used for crossing the stream. As the kingfisher skims along a foot or so above the water, it strikes the net and remains suspended in the clinging folds. I am in no way suggesting the destruction of these lovely creatures, but they can be taken alive in this manner in places where their presence is not permissible, and, there being always a ready sale for them for adorning ornamental and other waters, the disposal of any captured ones is easy and profitable.

CHAPTER XXV.

MOLES AND HOW TO CATCH THEM.

Opinions may be divided as to the merits of the mole, but there is no doubt that, under certain circumstances, it becomes a nuisance and has to be got rid of by some means or other, and the best means is to trap them. It is, however, necessary at the outset to point out that the natural history of the mole as popularly supplied is mostly incorrect. The mole's fortress as pictured and described is purely imaginative, and a good many other traits usually attributed to it are mainly incorrect.

For practical purposes it is enough to say that the mole becomes, under certain circumstances, not only a nuisance, but very damaging to farming interests, and also at times it is an undoubted fact that they become inimical to the interests of the game preserver.

Moles make two separate sets of tunnelings—permanent ones at depths varying from six inches to a foot or more beneath the surface, in connection with which is their nest or lair, and surface ones, mainly for the purpose of hunting their food. Very little, if any, soil is thrown out from the latter, the mole heaps of our fields, woods, and pastures coming from the deeper tunnels. It is in these latter that chief execution can be done when they are located at a sufficiently slight depth from the surface to be dealt with satisfactorily, but the surface runs also prove fruitful of catches when traps are put down in them within twelve, or at most twenty-four, hours after they are first made.

There are a large variety of mole traps manufactured and sold by various firms, almost all of which I have worked with from time to time, but although they all catch moles some of them possess disadvantages over the old-fashioned types which are in no way commensurate with other points they may possess.

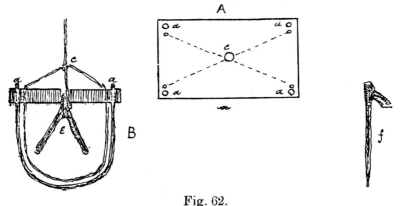

Fig. 62.

DETAILS OF SPRINGE MOLE TRAP.

For those possessing the time and slight ingenuity necessary, the ordinary springe mole trap, of which details are given at Figs. 62 and 63, is about as satisfactory as can be devised. It possesses the merit, moreover, that when a capture is effected the fact is made evident, and it saves an immense amount of trouble involved by wandering over the ground from trap to trap to discover whether any moles have been secured. At Fig. 62, a represents the cover, 5in. by 3in. and ½in. thick, with holes bored in it by augur and gimlet at the places shown. B shows a section of the cover with the trap set. Two pieces of split hazel are formed into bows and fitted securely at a a. Within their half-circle a wire noose is provided at each end of the cover, having its ends fastened together at c and attached to the line fixed to the bent hazel stick at d; e is a forked piece, which constitutes the trigger, and f illustrates some forked pegs 9in. long for holding the trap in position. Fig. 63 shows the trap set.

To set the trap effectually, having secured a site for it remove the covering from a portion of the mole run.

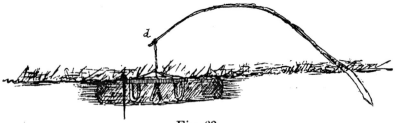

Fig. 63.

MOLE TRAP, SET.

Then, having adjusted the nooses as shown, make the cord secure through the central hole of the cover and plug it in position by means of the forked trigger (e). Now adjust the trap in position in the mole's run or tunnel and peg it securely down. In stiff soil two, in light soil four pegs will be required. Fix the hazel stick in position and bring down the end and adjust it to the cord of the trap. Then carefully cover and make all secure so as to prevent the ingress of light as far as possible into the run. The action of the trap is simple enough. The mole passing along its run displaces the trigger, the bowed stick flies up, and the victim is caught and killed by one or other of the wire nooses. It must be remembered that for its size the mole is remarkably strong, and goes very fast through its runs, passing easily at the rate of two yards a second through them, so that there is no need to be particular about setting the traps very "tickle."

The old pattern of iron-jawed mole trap is at best an unsatisfactory affair, but the principle is good, and em- bodied in latter-day patterns proves very serviceable. At Figs. 64 and 65 are illustrations of two thoroughly good forms of mole trap, which are far more easily set, and which possess the further merit of having the trigger piece attached to them, and so repeated loss of this important part is avoided. Insomuch that they are no more expensive than most of the old patterns and are far stronger, their advantage is manifest. Henry Lane is the maker.

Besides this form of mole trap there are others, upon what is known as the tunnel or barrel principle, but, frankly, if you cannot catch moles with the three traps described, you cannot do so with any others, and it would serve no good purpose to devote further time and space to them.

Moles are on the move at various times according to the weather, temperature, and season. They prefer deep tunneling in dry and frosty weather and surface work at others. Mole heaps are usually thrown up from the centre portions of a tunnel and not from the end, and by careful removal and examination the directions of the tunnels or runs can be ascertained. When dealing with deep runs, place one trap where the heap was, but be careful to clear out the run on each side before setting, and then endeavour to trace the run and place other traps upon other distinct portions of it.

When dealing with surface runs, choose freshly made ones, and place the traps a few feet from the end, as opposed to the beginning of them. What is known as a fern-trowel is the most useful tool to employ when mole catching. Weasels are frequently taken in mole runs, and the game preserver should carefully watch the

Fig. 64.   Fig. 65.

IMPROVED MOLE TRAP.   "SIMPLEX" MOLE TRAP.

neighbourhood of pheasants' and partridges' nests for mole workings. They frequently drive their tunnels beneath the actual nests, and either they or weasels abstract the eggs from below.

It is not very easy to become an expert mole catcher until you learn to discriminate between used and non-used runs and to grasp the drift of the mole's workings. Afterwards the matter becomes easy enough, and success in this direction is only a question of trouble and traps.

CHAPTER XXVI.

TRAPPING FISHERY PESTS.

There are one or two animals and birds which are extremely inimical at times to the interests of those working fisheries—trout, etc., rearing establishments— and controlling rivers and streams. Unless a stop be put to their depredations, much damage to stock, mature and immature, may occur, and it is therefore necessary to refer to them and the means of taking them in a concluding contribution.

Most notable amongst them is the otter, whose fame as a fish-destroyer has been made notorious, chiefly by those writers and others who possess very little actual knowledge of the subject. There are times when otters are actually most destructive to fish, but I am far from agreeing with the generally expressed opinion as to the habits of the otter, which gathers far more of its food on land than in the water. Anyone who may like to devote unprejudiced observation to the habits of this creature will soon become convinced of the accuracy of my contention. The time when otters are most destructive to fish is when they are educating their young, when they pursue precisely the same policy as we do when we are, say, educating a young gun-dog, and provide far more quarry for it than would be otherwise necessary. At the same time, otters have to be caught occasionally, and the manner of doing this must receive attention.

The otter for its size is a heavy and strong creature, often more than double the weight of a fox, and much more powerful. It requires a large and heavy trap to hold it, something after the style of Fig. 66, which shows the type of otter-trap proper. These traps have 6in. or 7in. jaws, a strong flat spring with setting ring, and an extra strong chain. Under certain circumstances the traps may require a much longer but less heavy chain up to 8ft. or 10ft. in length.

Some otter traps are fitted with spikes on the jaws, but this is a perfectly unnecessary adjunct. Nor should the spring be very hard-striking. I prefer immeasurably a supple, quick-striking one, but the jaws must hold very strongly, or the otter will escape.

Otters enter the water almost anywhere, but usually leave at certain regularly affected spots. These are usually shelving, and if sandy or muddy the seals of the paws can be easily made out. It is at such places that the otter can be trapped, and to succeed in doing so it is necessary to discover as many of these landing-places as possible, and provide each of them with traps, where promise is made that the otters are most likely to frequent them. Otters are most easily watched for and observed at dusk and at dawn, and, whatever their movements up and down the river or stream, it will be found that there are certain pools, ponds, and weirs which they mainly frequent, and it is at the shallows and sloping places at or adjacent to these spots that the otters both enter and leave the water most regularly.

The traps, if to take the otters alive, should have

short chains very securely and deeply staked, be placed
a yard or more at least from the water's margin, very
carefully covered, and left two or three days before
being considered ineffective or wrongly placed. It will
be quite possible to ascertain if the otter has passed
without getting into the trap, and, if so, do not move
the one already put down, but set another in the line
of the tracks shown.

If it be unnecessary to secure the otter alive, the

Fig. 66.

OTTER TRAP.

traps, provided with long chains, must be set close to the
water's edge or actually within its margin, if shallow
enough. In this case the otter when caught immediately seeks deep water and drowns. No bait is required for otter-trapping, but the traps require careful
lubricating. Fish oil may be employed for the purpose,
or vaseline, and the oiling should be thoroughly done
before the traps are employed. Otters possess a wonderfully keen scent, and newly-oiled traps are a hopeless
means against them.

Wherever otters frequent weirs or such places in

streams and rivers where the water runs over anything
in the nature of a weir in small volume, very favourable opportunity offers for securing them by using un-
covered traps. The great point, however, in regard to
otter-trapping is to discover their regular movements
first and work accordingly. It is very rarely that
young otters are caught in the same manner as the
parents, but if you take a bitch otter which has obviously got young, an ordinary large box-trap placed
beside the body of the mother and baited with a frog
or an eel will secure one or other of them.

I am so utterly opposed to the indiscriminate killing
of otters that I venture to repeat that, in my opinion, it
is only owners or controllers of fisheries who should
destroy or capture them as a preventive measure. They
do not do one-tenth the damage ascribed to them, and
to my mind to shoot or destroy an otter needlessly is a
gross and unpardonable offence.

One of the worst vermin of an ordinary trout-stream,
one of broken and tumbling water, such as exists in
endless number in these islands, is the poaching cat.
I have watched them over and over again and shot them
in their tracks, lying prone upon rock and bank, watching to dip out the unsuspecting fish, and have no doubt
that they are responsible for much damage to fish-rearing enterprises.

The heron is the one bird, probably, which does more
damage than anything else to fishery interests. At
every season it is destructive to fish in one form or
other, but, of course, most so when it destroys them on
the spawning beds and when full fish are working up
for spawning purposes. It is a bird of such long flight

that a heronry within ten miles or more of a stream is as likely to provide the source of damage as one alongside the water itself; and the fact that herons frequent a stream is in itself sufficient proof of their evil-doing. It is, of course, trout and grayling streams which suffer most, and where herons mainly forage.

They are not very difficult to trap once you fix upon their favourite fishing-places, and the best possible trap for them is the one shown at Fig. 67. It is a somewhat large and complicated affair, but very effective when

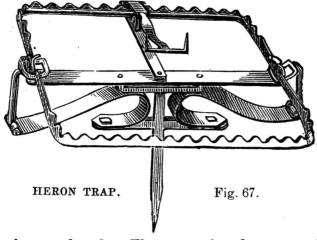

HERON TRAP. Fig. 67.

properly employed. The trap is always used under water, and must be placed in those positions where the birds have been noticed to do their fishing. The bait is a fish fixed upon the forked treadle, and to set the trap a couple of wooden wedges are necessary. They are introduced between the bottom of the frame of the trap and the top of the springs so as to enable the jaws to be opened and the catch adjusted. The trap is fixed upon the bed of the stream by means of the spike and

frame, with the head of the bait pointing upwards.
Any shallows, stickles, or runs, shelving bottom, etc.,
may be chosen as well as the tops of weirs and such
places where water runs thinly over any natural obstruction. The heron's movements, however, are the
best guide as to the situation to choose. It is just as
well to attach a long, thin chain to the trap, as, although caught round the head or neck and quickly

Fig. 68.

KINGFISHER TRAP.

killed, the birds sometimes flutter into deep water and
sink, trap and all.

I have already referred to the manner of taking king-
fishers in nets, but traps of the pattern shown at Fig. 68
can also be employed. These traps must be screwed or
clamped to any tree stumps, posts, etc., upon which the
birds are seen to alight from time to time, and be baited
with a small fish or simply be furnished with a small
perching-stick placed upon the forked trigger.

The kingfisher is such a charming bird that it is
greatly to be regretted that it is at times so destructive. It is to be hoped, however, that every excuse

may be made for their delinquencies, and only sheer necessity compel their destruction.

CONCLUDING REMARKS.

In the foregoing chapters it may be observed that no reference has been made to the trapping of badgers, a practice which obtains in some parts of the country, but has no sympathy of mine. For the same reasons no reference is made to owls, birds whose destruction or capture is wholly unwarranted, and which, but for the ignorance of gamekeepers and others, would never have suffered the depletion which their species have experienced.

Further, I have, whilst trying to make the work as comprehensive as possible, limited the references to traps which cover all possible requirements, without complicating matters by references to others of similar nature, but embodying the same principle. There is always quite a large number of new traps coming forward from time to time, meeting with some demand and then disappearing because they do not possess that particular value which commands permanent success. In a good many of them the theory is good ; practical application displays their weakness. In others the scope for their employment is so limited as to preclude their manufacture and sale under profitable conditions.

Finally, a few words as to the cruelty of trapping may not come amiss. Every true trapper endeavours to avoid the infliction of anything more than the necessary amount of pain on his victims. It is no use disguising the fact that the steel trap is a cruel instrument, but the amount of cruelty it inflicts is grossly exaggerated, and

I am convinced that it is this very exaggeration which has done more to hinder the adoption of humane methods than anything else. The professional trapper has been held up to so much odium that he has naturally put up his back and preferred to earn his living in the old way. There are abuses in every walk of life which embraces the taking of life, whether for purposes of food, sport, or necessity, but I have found that the skilled man is always the least cruel in his methods, and the bungler, from laziness or ignorance, the opposite.

No one who has done me the honour to follow me in what I have written will suggest that I have neglected to point out wherever possible where unnecessary cruelty can be avoided, and I would be the first to condemn any user of steel traps who allowed neglect of the details of his work, constant supervision of his tools and what they were doing, and the deliverance of his captures from their toils and pains at the very first moment practicable to creep into his work. The man who sets a trap and deliberately or by accident forgets all about it is grossly to blame. In the same way, one who discovers that one or more of his traps have been broken away from their fastenings or stake, and presumably carried or drawn off by the animal taken, should not cease from hunting for them until they are found and the victim released.

It is more by sins of omission than commission that unnecessary cruelty is caused in the using of steel traps. The day is I am afraid, still, far off when we shall be able to dispense with them, and in the meantime it behoves everyone employing them to do so with the greatest limitation of their pain-inflicting powers that is possible under the circumstances.

INDEX.

Box-traps, 143
  Illustrations of, 144, 145, 147, 151
  Double-ended, 145
  Open-ended, 148
  Open-fronted, 151
  Simple form of, 144

Cage-traps, 143, 152, 153
Cats, wild, 97
  Poaching, 102
  Baits for, 105
  Hugger traps for, 103
Chains for steel traps, 6, 10, 41
Clap-nets, 199
Clifford's traps, 186
Collapsible steel traps, 13
  Illustrations of, 13, 14
Concluding remarks, 223
Crows, trapping, 129

Deadfall trap, 148, 186
Deadfalls, 180
Dogs, poaching, 102
  Traps for, 103
  Baits for, 105
Dorset trap, 4
  Collapsible (Lane's), 13
  Description of parts, 4
  Detachable springs for, 12
  How to set the, 22
  Humane forms of, 15
  Illustrations of, 7, 10, 11, 12
  Improved, 11, 12
  Main points in, 4
  Ordinary, the, 10, 21
  Stakes for, 8
  Variations of the, 9

Everitt's patent trap, 90
  Illustrations of, 90, 91

Figure-of-four trap, 181
Fishery pests, 217
Foxes, 107

Foxes,
  Baits for, 115
  Humane traps for, 116
  Trapping, 107
  Traps for, 109

General trapping hints, 32
General trapping and snaring, 178
Ground Game Act, 45
  Position of " occupier " using traps
    under, 46
Ground vermin, 60
  Trapping, 61
  Traps for, 61
  The polecat, 62
  The stoat, the weasel, 66, 67

Handling caught rabbits, 61
Hares,
  Snares for, 173
  How to snare, 174
Hawks,
  Baits for, 121
  Taking young, 125
  The sparrow-hawk, 121
  Trapping, 120
  Traps for, 122
Herons, 220
  Trap for, 221
Hingles 190
  Illustrations of, 191
Humane traps, 15, 18
  Mitchell's patent, 16
  Round, 37
  Sara's patent, 18
  With flat jaws, 17
Hugger traps, 35

Illustrations,
  Box-traps, 144, 146, 148, 151
  Cage-traps, 153
    Clifford's, 155, 156
    Plan and section of, 154

Illustrations,
  Clap-net, 200
    Brace for play-bird, 204
    Play-bird for, 203
  Dead-fall traps, 148, 186
  Dorset traps, 7, 10, 11
  Double-spring vermin trap, 146
  Everitt's patent trap, 92
  Egg-eating bird trap, 139
  Figure-of-four trap, 181, 183
  Folding vermin trap, 39
  Funnel cage-trap, 160
  Hawk-trap, plain, 35
    ,,   toothed, 36
  Heron-trap, 221
  Humane fox-trap, 118
  Idstone pit-trap, 157
    Plan of, 158
    Section of, 157
  Improved Dorset traps, 23
  Iron stakes for traps, 50
  Lane's collapsible trap, 13, 14
  Mole-traps, 214, 216
  Ordinary Dorset traps, 23
  Out-o'-sight trap, 96
  Otter-trap, 219
  Pen-trap, 161, 162
  Pennsylvania trap, 97
  Pitfall, 188
  Pull-up action in traps, 36
  Rabbit's foot-marks, 50
  Rabbit-snares, 166, 168
  Rabbit-nets, 209
  Round trap with rubber jaws, 37
  Sara's humane trap, 19, 20
  Single-spring vermin-trap, 40
  Stop-thief trap, 94
  Springes, 191, 192, 193
  Tunnel cage-trap, 160
  Tunnel-traps, 208
  Wire rat-trap, 95
  Wire spring-trap, 12
Improved Dorset traps, 11
Introductory remarks on trapping, 1

Jays, 133
  Baits for, 135
  Habits of, 137
  Trapping, 133
  Traps for, 137

Killing down rabbits, 48
Kingfishers,
  Nets for, 213
  Traps for, 225

Lamp for trapping at night, 59
Lane's collapsible trap, 13
  Illustrations of, 13, 14

Magpies, 133
  Baits for, 135
  Habits of, 136
  Trapping, 133
  Traps for, 139
Mitchell's humane trap, 16
  Do.   do.   adaptor, 16
  Illustrations of, 16
Moles, 212
  Traps for, and illustrations, 213,
    214, 216

Nets, 199
  Clap-nets, 199
    How to set, 201
    Illustration of, 200
    Play-bird for, 203
  Drop-nets, 205
  Glade-nets, 210
  Long-nets, 209
  Rabbit-nets, 208
  Trailing, 209
  Tunnel-nets, 207
    Plan of, 208
  For kingfishers, 211

Pen-trap, 162
Pitfalls, 187
  Illustration of, 188
  Barrel, 189
Poaching dogs and cats, 104
Polecat, the 64
  Habits of, 66
  Haunts of, 65
  Trapping, 66
Pull-up action in traps, 35
  ,,   trigger-traps, 36

Rabbits, 25, 47
Rabbit-trapping, 26, 47
  Along hedgerows, 56
  Choosing the ground for, 53
  Choice of sites for traps, 57
  Covering the traps, 51
  Footmarks of rabbits, 49
  How to tell well-worked runs, 57
  Handling caught rabbits, 61
  In spring-time, 48
  Moving traps, 60
  Movements of rabbits, 58
  Quantity of traps required, 54
  Traps working badly, 59, 60

Rabbit trapping, times for, 57
Resetting traps, 59
Season for, 53
Visiting traps, 58
Rabbit-snaring, 163
Making snares, 166
Illustrations of, 166, 168
Rats, 76
Baits for. 85
Game and, 89
Trapping of, general, 79
,, in buildings, 90
,, in fields, 86
,, in woods, 82
Traps for, 92, 94, 95, 96, 97
Snares for, 176
Raven, the, 127
Round traps, 34
Chains for, 43
Forked treadles for, 44
How to employ, 43
,, set, 42
Rook, the, 127
Trapping, 131

S-hooks for traps, 10
Sara's humane trap, 18, 19
Setting round traps, 44
Small vermin-traps, 45
Rabbit-traps, 50
Small steel-traps, 39
How to set, 42
Stakes (iron) for, 41
Snares, 163
Illustrations of, 166, 168
Making, 164
Stakes for, 165
Use of, generally, 169
Do. for hares, 170
Snares, small, 175
For rats, 177
Snaring, times for, 171
Birds, 178
Poaching dogs and cats, 179
Stakes for traps, 8
How to make. 8
Sparrow-hawk, 121
Springs for traps, 12
Wire traps, 12
Detachable 12
Springes, 190
Bow, 193
Materials for, 195
Ordinary, 190, 191
Post and rail, 194, 195
Stoats, habits of, 68, 69

Stoats, baits for, 73, 75
Trapping, 70

Tools for trapping, 21
Illustrations of, 23
Trapper, the, maxims for, 32
Trapping, remarks on, 1
Crows 129
Foxes, 113
General, and snaring, 178
Ground vermin, 62
Hawks, 120
Herons, 221
Jays, 133
Magpies, 133
Moles 215
Otters, 220
Rooks, 131
Rabbits, 26
Rats, 92, 93, 94, 95
Winged vermin, 120
Traps,
Box, 143, 146, 148
Trigger for, 147
Burgess' patent, 17
Cage, 153, 155
Clifford's, 156
Dorset, 4
Deadfall, 148, 186
Figure-of-four, 181, 183
Grades of, 9
Humane, 15, 18
Hugger, 35
Illustrations of (see under "I")
Idstone, 157
Kingfisher, 222
Mitchell's humane, 16
Mitigating, 15
Pen, 162
Round and small, 34
Sara's humane, 18

Varieties of Dorset traps, 9
Vermin, ground, 60
,, winged, 120

Weasels, habits of, 69
Baits for, 73, 75
Trapping, 70
Winged vermin, 120
Wire-spring traps, 12
Wire cage-trap, 154
Wild cats, 99
Habits of, 101
Trapping, 102
Woodcocks, 197

LONDON :

PRINTED AT THE OFFICES OF THE "SHOOTING TIMES AND BRITISH
SPORTSMAN," 72-77 TEMPLE-CHAMBERS, FLEET-STREET, E.C.

Lightning Source UK Ltd.
Milton Keynes UK
UKOW03n1541230914

239045UK00002B/5/A